MA

Presents

PSALMS FROM THE HILLS of WEST VIRGINIA

by
JANET HURLOW

Foreword by
Sister Marie Carol Hurley

Preface by
Matthew Fox O.P.

BEAR & COMPANY
The Publishers of Creation-Centered Spirituality
6 Vista Grande Court
Santa Fe, New Mexico 87501

Dedicated with Love to God, His Earth Children, and all his Creation

Bear & Company Books are published by Bear & Company, Inc. Its Trademark, consisting of the words "Bear & Company" and the portrayal of a bear, is Registered in U.S. Patent and Trademark Office and in other countries. Marca Registrada Bear & Company, Inc., 6 Vista Grande Court, Santa Fe, New Mexico 87501. PRINTED IN THE UNITED STATES OF AMERICA

Cover art copyright © 1982 by Bear & Company, Inc.

COPYRIGHT © 1982 by Bear & Company, Inc.
ISBN 0-939680-04-1
Library of Congress Card Number

All rights reserved. No part of this book may be reproduced by any means and in any form whatsoever without written permission from the publisher.

Bear & Company, Inc.
6 Vista Grande Court
Santa Fe, NM 87501

Calligraphy by: Lynden H. Galloway
Cover and Interior Design—Bill Davenport and Peter McKelvey Shea
Front cover photograph— Peg Reynolds, C.S.J.
Typography—Grand Design, Santa Fe, NM
Printed in the United States by Banta Company

FOREWORD

Wild, wonderful West Virginia, a place of surprising beauty and beautiful surprises! Among the most beautiful and surprising—Janet Hurlow and her books.

Janet appeared at our first Scripture sharing in a small West Virginia town—with all her family. Her gentle eyes never left me as I read from the Scriptures and we spoke about them. Her insights into the Word of God were beautiful—and surprising too.

At each sharing Janet was there; sometimes with her sister, Vivian, almost as shy as Janet, often with her pleasant, quiet husband, Okey. They seemed to be so moved by the Scripture, so responsive to the sharing. We became friends without exchanging many words. Each time we tried to do something for Janet, she outdid us in generosity. We shared some clothing; she painted us a beautiful portrait of Jesus. We drove her home from an evening session, and there was Okey at the door of the trailer with a dozen fresh mountain eggs.

It was on that evening that I asked her, "Janet, who taught you so much about the Bible?"

"Well," she replied, "My Gramma Day raised me. She taught me the 'Our Father' and that if you have two coats and someone needs one, you give him one of yours. I've always tried to do that."

One evening she and Vivian approached me timidly with three large ledger-type books. "Sister, would you read my books?"

"Janet! You've written three books!"

"Well," Vivian said, "Janet doesn't exactly write them herself."

"Oh," I asked, "did you help her?"

"No. A kind of glow appears on the pages and I see the words and sort of copy them." Janet explained quietly.

3

That frightened me a bit. I'm so skeptical and rational. I would have been interested in the poetry of a simple West Virginian woman like Janet, but "light on pages" and "messages from a higher source" were not for me. But I loved Janet so I took the books; when she had gone I sat down and began to read.

I encountered a strange sort of script with no punctuation (reproduced on pages   and   ). It was not easy at first, but then beautiful phrases began to emerge from the pages!

> Such love, such kindness is in God . . . Father is His title . . .
> gentle is His way . . . Blessed is His playful spirit . . . Ease
> into virtue naturally.

I read further; I could scarcely believe the beauty of the messages I was reading. I called my preaching partner, Fr. Martin Iott. "Marty, come read Janet's books."

For hours we sat reading aloud to one another. We called the Pastor, Father Raymond, who listened for a while and then took up a book, too.

"Listen to this!" one would say. We were enraptured with "This is the saints of God who speak. This is the inhabitants of another world filled with wonder and mystery for earth." "Signs of joy are on earth when mankind shares God's blessing." "Each spirit that sings is God's own dear child."

About 1:30 a.m. I went to bed but was scarcely able to sleep. Next morning we went to visit Janet in her tiny trailer. The three youngest children were home from school with an infection.

We fired question after question at poor Janet. Her replies were so direct, so simple.

"When did you write these books, Janet?"

"It was in September, 1973. I'd been writing down questions that came to mind. One day I closed my eyes and moved my pen and when I looked words appeared on the page."

"What did they say?"

"It was a sort of greeting, like 'How are you?' At first I began to get parts of sentences and directions. This was in printing."

"How did you feel?"

"I was so stunned I went to Vivian and she told me to keep on writing. I soon found the words were on the page. There was like a glow on the page around them and I could copy them easily. The writing became clearer. It changed from printing to writing."

"To this script?"

"Yes. I was told to begin all the messages 'In the Name of the Father and of the Son and of the Holy Spirit.' I believe that was to assure me the messages were from a good source, not an evil source."

"Why did you get these books?"

"Vivian bought the books because I was told there would be books."

"Where do you think the messages come from?"

"I'm not certain. Some names appeared. I only know they are not from me. They come from a higher source."

"Did you tell anyone about them?"

"I tried to tell the Holy Father, Pope Paul, but I don't believe he got the letter. Then I gave the books to Fr. Raymond for protection. It's hard to keep things from the children here in this small trailer. See, Mark and Lisa have scribbled on some pages."

I could see they had. The whole thing was a beautiful paradox, like many of Jesus' parables—the profound messages in simple, old-fashioned, repetitive phrases, some marred by children's crayon scribbling. A treasure of richest wisdom in a trailer with only two chairs. The marvelous humor of God to bring this treasure to us!

"The messages are for the whole world. Will you help me share them?"

Why not? We are told that Catherine of Siena, Our Dominican Sister, was taught to read and write by teachers not of this earth. God always has chosen the least, the small ones.

God's spirit reaches out to children of a small kind, and all inspirations must be kept small so man will understand.

So we began to share the "books"—"Janet's Books." Each person we shared them with was touched. They spoke of the peace, the comfort the messages brought them. They wanted copies. We knew a right way must be found to get the message of "God's kindness and love for little earth children" to others. We were reading Father Matthew Fox's books at that time, and it seemed to us that Janet's messages were speaking of the same "creation spirituality" he is writing about—speaking of the same kind, gentle Father he finds and we find in the words of Jesus. So we brought the

5

books to him. We even brought Janet to him. That was a big step on the way.

The other steps were equally wild and wonderful. All the preparation was a gift...Carmine, the level-headed realist, with matter of factness, giving with unrealistic generosity the equipment, material, time, and secretary. And Donna, inspired by the messages, made the pages a work of art. So much care...so much sharing...so much love. Janet's messages inspiring all of us, each one of us so different. But there it is!

All men see differently.
See as you wish and love in your special spirit.
You who see beauty, see beauty.
You who see great meanings, see great meanings.
Take God's gifts!

Now Janet would like to share her books with all of us poor little earth children.

Sister Marie Carol Hurley

PREFACE

This book of Psalms is both ordinary and extraordinary. It is ordinary for its simplicity, its wide appeal, its timeliness, its beauty, and its truthfulness. It is extraordinary for the same reasons. These Psalms are for all of us, parent and child, theologian and factory worker, musician and carpenter, follower of Moses, Jesus, or Buddha. They were first brought to my attention because, as the bearer of the gift explained, they seemed to put into poetry the prayer of praise that marked the creation-centered spirituality I write about as a spiritual theologian. And they do. These Psalms announce the Glad Tidings of old that have been so often muddled over: That life, all of creation, is a beautiful gift intended for our enjoyment and sharing of the enjoyment. So simple a message. And, today, so extraordinary.

These Psalms sing of the end of a spiritual era that has confused war with art and asceticism with spirituality. Therefore, these Psalms sing of a new spiritual era. Instead of the art of war this book praises the art of living that alone makes for peacefulness within and among peoples. Instead of war, for example, between body and soul this book anounces the beauty of the marriage of earth and spirit.

> Righteous ones enjoy what pleasures the body
>   craves in God's Love.
> Speak of the needs of the spirit, and speak
>   of the body's needs.
> Combine your pleasures so well.
> This is the way.

Instead of a war between this life and life-after-death, this book proclaims the truth that eternal life has already begun.

> Come walk in the cool meadows of God's Love and
>   refresh at the springs of eternal life.

Blessed ones, Heaven is a spiritual song sung
in living spirits.

Life is sacred.
Kind ones, in God is life with no end.

Instead of bemoaning the Fall, it sings of the beauty of creation.

Earth, earth, God is your creator!
O such a blessed creator!
So very in order is our earth creation.
Blessed is our God who fashioned her and
molded us in His sacred image.
Come, see such a God!

Instead of putting persons down by counting their sins, it speaks
the truth of one another's beauty.

In such beauty as man has never seen he
develops as an earth child from a seed in
the womb of its mother, becomes so beautiful
And never stops in this beauty.

All such beauty is yours.

All persons are made in God's image.

Children are songs, Songs of God.
Each one has his songs written in his spirit.
Sing as sweetly as you desire.

Instead of puny moralisms that put people in their place, these
Songs challenge and release people to divine bigness.

God is your destination
Such beauty fills your spirit!
It is your song, and love has no limit!
Go as far as you wish.

Virtuous Spirits, God shall give you himself,
And more than this does not exist.

Spirit of earth, seek your God.
See the limitless wonders of His love.

Instead of moral and religious elitism, every person is called to
develop his or her God-like beauty and spacefulness.

Why settle for less?
God wants your splendor, your individuality,
your only special self!
So rich shall your nature grow.

So much shall you be yourself and so pleased
in God in your spiritual beauty.

Each one is called.
Here is wisdom: a creator fashions his beings and speaks
in each one.

Children, God desires your beauty.
As you sing, so shall you live forever.

Instead of encouraging a mortification of senses, this book delights
in God's shapes and scents and sounds.

In all the earth is a glorious perfume sent out from God,
Sent forth in God's Love.
Songs of the saints bless with the freshness of the
morning dew,
Bless with the sweetness of roses and wild flowers.

Instead of confusing art with commercial entertainment or the
selling of objects or the collections of the wealthy, this book speaks
the truth: that beauty is everywhere and everyone's.

Earth people who should understand are so foolish.
Come, put away your foolish ways.
All such beauty is yours.

Instead of introvert meditation, extrovert concentration on God-
made beauties.

Such wonders are in God's creations!
Bless such a God who sets such a mighty
world in peace and order,
Rest and beauty such as you cannot conceive
are in God's spirit.

Such lovely beings filled with music and rest!
Seen are the things of God.
Under many suns, in many galaxies.
Such things are real and seen soon.

Instead of the violence and control of our present era, we are led to
express gentleness to all God's creatures.

Kindness is a gift from the Holy Spirit.
God sends her so beautifully into the
souls of the saints.
This is a kind gentle song God sends to men who seek
her beauty.
So sweet and special is kindness.

Keep her in your heart, speak to her, sign
her name on her Father's creation.

Instead of sentimentalism, angry criticism that includes criticism of greed, materialistic consumerism and luxury living.

Cry, O people who buy and spend.
There is only one God and soon you shall see.
Wisdom is not in the money purse or in fine
cloth and rich laces.
Wisdom is not in a well-set table or luxury
or the clashing of metal.
Wisdom is in God and his treasures.
Mankind is yet to see.

And we are chided for forgetting our bonds to holy nature and creation.

Why are you mourning, O beautiful world, who
once laughed and sang in the sun early
in the dawn of creation?
You mourn not because of your age.
This is not the reason.
Is it because your children have turned
against you and your creator?
Yes, this is the sadness seen.
And where is your brother the sun and your
sister the moon?
The sun blushes and hides her face.
O God, she is so ashamed.
And the moon rises up in earth's behalf,
but she is so small.
O moon, you shall not be small and bare forever.

Instead of a distant and foreboding theistic diety, we are shown the nearness and intimacy of a pantheistic God.

In all things is our God.

God is so near
Heaven is open.

Why are you so sad, beings of earth?
God is still singing in creation.
Our God is so wonderful!

God is freedom.
In his love, rest.

Our God, most delighted are we with you!
Come fill our spirits with your love.
Sing with us in this beautiful garden, and
   run and play among the flowers with us.

Instead of earthly chauvinism, a reverence and respect for all of the universe.

Vast is God's creation.
Small is earth in this creation.
So small is earth in the Father's setting.
God is the maker of other worlds.

Instead of introverted withdrawal from the universe, a challenge from the cosmos.

In such beauty is our cosmos created.
In God is all beauty.
We, in God's spirit, spirits righteous and true,
   wait for the day when our brothers and sisters of earth
   who are in God's spirit shall come into our world of
   sweet music.
Eat the fruit and drink the wine of
   worlds you do not know exist.
Children of earth, children of the cosmos,
   in one spirit, rest.

Instead of famous names buttressed by fancy positions and gigantic academic institutions, the smallness of a mountain lady reminding us of the democracy of God.

In all earth never was such a
Book written by such a small one as writes;
Which is why she writes.
The smallest is as important as the great
   and mighty, and the great and mighty as the
   smallest.

And finally a word for the reader.

Earth, Earth, when will her little ones
   become wise?
What will it take to make them see?

It seems to be that with a book as simple, as prayerful, as promiseful, and as truthful as this, our blindness might be cured and we might all see once again. It has been my privilege to meet the simple mystic who has lent us these Psalms. Her joyful spirit in the midst of daily struggle for survival is ample evidence of the specialness of these poems. Some people will demand to know where they come from but we do not know enough yet about the energies of the universe or of human nature to label their origins as paranormal, psychic, angelic, human, or divine. Most probably, they are born of a happy blending of all such energies since God's grace builds on nature and works through nature. The reader should enter into the book and learn from it and not be distracted by the mysteriousness of its origins. It was born of a simple and good mountain lady, a woman poorer in this world's goods than the vast majority of Americans.

What we can affirm with certainty is the soundest test ever offered for any claims to the extraordinary: "By their fruits you shall know them." If the fruits of these Psalms are to return us to creation and to the beauty and justice that the Creator intended; if people who read them return to peaceful, compassionate living; then that is all we need to know about them. Instead of wasting energy in idle curiosity, we need to say, "Thank you, mountain lady, for these gifts—wherever they are from Thank you for replacing ascetic spirituality with aesthetic spirituality, one that finds beauty everywhere. Thank you for replacing a pessimistic, introspective, redemption outlook with dreams of the grace-filled, God-filled theologians, more poetically than preachers, more universally than statesmen, more urgently than politicians. For this is the role—the prophetic role—of the bona fide mystic in deeply troubled times: to lead us from despair, nihilism, and violence to blessing, creativity, and harmonious living. This theology of blessing—so rich in the creation-spirituality of the Hebrew Bible and the New Testament—is the Good News that this book calls us back to.

Blessedness is what God wills.
O, sweet, kind little ones: Come
To God's very blessed and wonderful world.

Matthew Fox
Institute in Creation-Centered
Spirituality
Mundelein College, Chicago

Psalms
from the Hills
of
West Virginia

Sound the good news Sound the good
news in all the Earth is the call. Sound
out a special message sons of God
in such peace is the call. Sing a song
of peace and love, this Earth is soon
to see God in all his splendor. Sound
out very Sounds of joy an inspirational
spirit sings her song make merry
all you people of Earth Spread the
Spirit of peace, Earth sings To her
Creator now is a Time of Times
while inspirational music fills
the Earth God Spirit inspires
you so sweetly come in Gods peace,
you very wise Spirits Earth is now
in her last Blessed State Come
make this a time Each Child
Who Rests shall Sing Blessedly
with God very same Songs as
the Saints of Special quality
Sing such music fills the
Earth and Heavens in Gods
inspirational beauty
Blessings are on Gods Children
Such Special Blessings Very Blessed
Children in Gods Spirit in Gods
Spirit are his Saints in Gods
Spirit is life, Rest and peace Rightious
Spirits Sound Out the news Sound
out Gods Blessed peace and love Amen.

God instructs all the wise

God instructs all the wise.
And virtue sings in children who wait in God's Love.
Blessed saints, start your prayers in the Blessed Trinity.
In the name of the Father and of the Son and of the Holy Spirit,
Amen.

Start each message in the same manner.
This is wise.

Children of earth, blessed of God,
Children of God come.
Start all life's undertakings in God's name.
Come in God's Love.
Start a kind song.
Such is God's way and such singing blesses earth.
So wisely, rest,
In God's Love
Amen.

Sound the good news

Sound the good news!
Sound the good news!
In all the earth is the call.
Sound out a special message, Sons of God.
In such peace is the call.
Sing a song of peace and love!
This earth is soon to see God in all his splendor!
Sound out very sounds of joy.
An inspirational spirit sings her song.
Make merry all you people of earth.
Spread the spirit of peace.
Earth sings to her creator.
Now is the time of times.
While inspirational music fills the earth,
God's spirit inspires you so sweetly.
Come, in God's peace, you very wise spirits,
Come, make this a time.
Each child who rests shall sing blessedly with God,
The very same song as the saints of special quality
    sing.
Such music fills the earth and heavens in God's
    inspirational beauty.
Blessings are on God's children,
Such special blessings!
Very blessed children in God's spirit,
In God's spirit are his saints,
In God's spirit is life, rest and peace.
Righteous spirits sound out the news
Sound out God's blessed peace and love!
Amen.

O mighty

O mighty,
O this God is the most inspiring God,
Filled with such singing, such interests.
Blessed God, righteous and so very beautiful,
Filled with such a song!
You righteous, ease into God's way naturally.
Such is God's way.
Virtue is a natural interesting way,
Ease of mind under no pressure.
Rest comes in this way.
As you make one sacrifice keep in God's Love.
See a wonderous adventure.
See a time as you reach in God's understanding.
Never have you seen such understanding and gentleness
    as is this God of ours.
You are in for such a surprise!
At this very time while earth is in full bloom,
    God calls.
So while you arrive God's spirit overflows in your
    spirit.
Come, earth children, make yourselves full of life
    and good times!
Live so well in God's Love!
In this state you remain so blessedly,
Laughing and singing to God with such joy and peace!
This is the way God wants you.
This is the way you shall arrive.
This is the only state of blessed singing you are to
    come in, blessed of earth!
Amen.

The time has come to use your gifts

The time has come to use your gifts.
Please God, earth children, in all your ways.
Please him.
Sing with the Love of God.
Instruct so wisely.
Pray so blessedly.
Play and work in God's Love,
With wisdom in your spirits.
Bless in God's name.
Touch and heal nations who are weary and sick
Who are blind and who are poor.
Come.
God calls each one in his love.
Come, children,
See the morning sun.
Sing out, you who are sick and in such agony of spirit and body.
Kindness comes in God's Love.
She brings in fruit from Christ's bounty that all might be fed.
Many in this earth sing in such kind spirits,
In such sweet kind spirits.
Some shall instruct from this very book.
And many shall listen.
Are you inspired?
So very inspired are many!
Amen.

Sing on earth in God's Love

Sing on earth in God's Love.
Soon you shall sing in God's presence in God's Kingdom.
God is such a virtuous spirit.
Kindness sings blessed gentle songs.
In this book are God's signs.
Come, rest, kind spirit.
Rest and keep kindness.
You are now called children,
Blessed children of earth.
Soon in such spirit
God calls you with a father's love.
So gentle is God, so desirable,
No man could reject him,
If he knew the very nature of God's spirit.
Such peace rests in such beauty.
O sons of men, is our spirit of God?
Is this an inspirational message from God's Kingdom?
Set your hearts at ease.
In God's spirit rests your spirit.
Nothing soothes and takes away fears as complete trust in God.
Songs of blessed peace fill each heart and comfort each soul.
In God's singing is life with no end.
In God's singing is comfort in all ways.
Such beautiful music makes a kind, blessed earth.
Amen.

God is in your spirit

God is in your spirit.
You who rise in the morning
Singing his love song in this earth,
In the morning before the dawn.
Start each blessed day in God's Love, singing
And remembering God's beauty.
In peace may rest come to man.
In God's Love remembering such a time in God's spirit.
Keep blessed the time.
It is a sweet and sacred time when no sorrow shall reach you.
In God's spirit is such peace.
Make a start in kindness.
Sing in the presence of God.
Let nothing make you stop trying.
Keep in God's presence.
Sing out so very wisely.
God understands all your needs.
Ask, little spirits!
Ask God in all ways.
Reach out in God's service.
Kindness blesses all who seek her.
Inspire, instruct, bless, righteous spirits.
Rest, earth children, on this earth.
Bless with such kindness;
Reach out.
Many souls need your spirits.
Many shall see.
Many are called.
While earth waits, come all you who rest in God's Love.
Righteous in spirit,
Very spirit of God,
You arrive in God's Love,
Blessed and pure.
Amen.

Speak out, small ones.

21

Speak out, small ones.
God hears the voice of even the smallest.
His ears are attentive to the worst sinners.
His spirit reaches to the densest forest.
His spirit heals and comforts the pagan child.
His voice calls out to the wildest beast, and
    his mercy comforts its young.
He sees the ways of all beings,
From the smallest to the largest,
From the weakest to the strongest,
From the wisest to the most foolish.
Come all of you.
Sing a love song in earth.
God is so sacred.
Sing of His Love in all your ways.
Take this wisdom.
God's spirit blesses his saints.
In God's Love.
Amen.

Pride has no room in this chosen race of earth

Pride has no room in this chosen race of earth children.
Cast her out.
Sing a small song.
Most delightful is your smallness in God's spirit.
Songs of such beauty fill the Heavens.
Start a song to God in earth.
Keep singing.
Blessed is your song of life.
In God's spirit rest your case.
In God's Love.
Amen.

Blessed saints in earth's toil

Blessed saints in earth's toil,
Most merciful is your Father.
Bring your gifts with songs of love and
thanksgiving.
Sorrow shall be turned into great joy.
Why are you so sad?
Why do you cry?
In such a short while your sorrows are over.
Soon is singing heard where sorrow signed her
name.
So sacred is life.
Saints keep seeking her richness in earth's
sorrow.
God's spirit sings of life, such as earth
children have never known.
Come here, small ones.
See life!
In its true nature, walk.
God's spirit is very much alive.
All earth is small.
Could this be life?
So kind is our God to give life to such
small creatures.
His spirit sings so well to men of earth
who stay in His Love.
Come, share with us such wonders of life.
Earth is only a fragment of such wonders.
See such things as interest man.
From God's spirit flows life without limit.
Take all the richness and beauty desired by
man.
God comes in wisdom, His understanding is all
wise.
To lift man out of the things he knows is
not part of God's plans.
Understand this.
Receive life more abundantly.
In God's Love.
Amen.

Books sent to earth are sent with love

Books sent to earth are sent with love.
Sent to serve man's needs while he is in
    earth's toil.
Each word is sent in God's spirit to heal
    and comfort God's children.
In such a sorrowful time in earth be so
    thankful, small ones.
God has not left you alone in earth.
Seek God's spirit.
All you people of earth, sing a love song
    that will never end.
So so wise.
Blessed are you, earth, in God's spirit,
And your blessings will never end.
God is pleased with such children, who
    bless earth in his spirit.
Songs of life are in God's saints.
Each one blesses and heals so well in
    union with God's spirit.
In earth you were created.
In earth your spirit played and danced in
    God's creation.
God sang to you so sweetly.
Sang a love song to an earth spirit.
Your blessings come in God's love.
Beings of earth, so wise, remain as you are,
    earth creatures in God's creation.
Come close, very sorrowful ones,
Come close.
It is earth who comes in God's Love.
Welcome earth.
In God's Love.
Amen.

This is why you were created.
Sing as you desire, beloved spirits of earth.
Soon God rests everyone who sings in his
    spirit.
Children of God, come take your blessings.
Earth is in your spirits.
This is earth.
These are her children.
She is seen in each one.
Most delightful spirits, reach Heaven so
    well.
Right you are to seek earth's pleasures.
It is in your spirits to seek such delights.
This is our spiritual sign.
Sing a pleasant song while you wait.
Sing in God's spirit and slip not from his
    precepts.
Seek no pleasure above him.
This is his desire: that your journey be
    enjoyable.
Do good, avoid evil, sing a sacred song,
    and understand God does not send your
    sorrow.
There is an evil in the earth that is against
    God.
In God's Love.
Amen.

Holy spirit sent from the Father   25

Holy spirit sent from the Father, song of
     never ending life,
From your spirit are spirits created.
Earth beings bless their God so well.
Would you sing in each one?
God is pleased with such goodness.
Without her no man would be saved.
Sorrow is in the earth.
But God is so kind.
In this be wise.
Without a virtuous spirit man cannot
     come to God's sweet care.
Such music takes mankind to God in song
     of unending beauty.
Kiss of sacredness in all things!
To each is given his own way of seeing.
O such blessings are on the spirit that
     can see God's wonders in everything
     created.
Virtue does not limit her spirit.
Within each breast she sings a different
     song.
So lovely is her music!
Mankind could not stand in her presence
     in his lowly nature.
In God's Love.
Amen.

Such love of all things is in the heart.
Such things as you see hold beauty as the
    spirit sings to the body
Of such wonders as God has made.
Songs of such beauty come not to all men.
This is your gift, small ones.
You see as your spirit whispers.
Beauty comes from within your being.
Sing with the beauty of the earth.
This is a gift of virtue.
It is in this wisdom you were born.
In worlds without end virtue sings an
    unending song of beauty.
All who are in God's spirit see with one
    spirit.
See as we are created to see.
Speak of the beauty in your spirit, but
    do not expect interest in your sweet
    joy of life.
Some come seeing.
Others cannot see.
Some see less,
Others see more,
Some see things you cannot see,
And you see as others do not see.
This is the nature of man.
In Christ's spirit is true joy.
See the wonders of God in a clean
    spirit, so that you may see more fully.
Live in peace with all creation.
True beauty comes from a spirit filled with
    the Holy Spirit.
In God's Love.
Amen.

Here is your song sung in God's spirit

Here is your song sung in God's spirit forever.
In this song is blessed life.
Love is the way to God.
Love has no limit.
All other virtue rests in her wisdom.
Understand this.
Here is such music born.
There is a spiritual gift that reaches
    beyond the senses of man.
With pure delicate notes she is sung
    in creation.
In worlds signs of love are reached
    beyond mankind's understanding.
This is where the earth begins.
Where our desires rest.
God's spirit is the source of love.
Spirits are bathed in her.
She is in earth beings who reach out
    to God.
O sweet pure streams of love coming
    from the Father, flood the spirits of
    man.
Bathe us in your pure essence.
Sweetness of life takes us away and
    we sing before God in your beauty
    forever.
In God's Love.
Amen.

28 God blesses all who reach out for his love

God blesses all who reach out for his love.
In God's Love find peace.
In God's Love is all peace.
The true spirit of peace comes from God.
There is no peace in things of earth's craving.
Spend your time in God's Love.
And you shall understand.
This is earth,
In her wisdom she comes in many ways.
While you seek her treasures, she seeks God.
This is.
Children of God use earth's treasures in God's Love.
God sends all good things to those who love him.
So use the many gifts of earth in God's Love.
All you children so wise, so understanding,
Praising God in blessing you with all things!
So he pleases in all ways.
Earth children serve God.
This is where peace makes her home.
Peace is with all who live in God's Love.
This is God's Way,
And you who please God
Who place God above earth's gifts,
Shall come to enjoy all things in peace.
Sing out in all things!
Sing as children in delightful spirits.
Accepting all gifts as from God
While you wait.
Amen.

Sing, righteous little children

Sing, righteous little children!
God wishes you all good things.
Spend your time wisely, spirits of God;
Receiving in God's Love and giving with much love,
Remembering who gives in such love so blessedly,
Remembering where peace makes her sweet abode.
This is a special kind of people who never forget where all
    good things are from.
God is pleased in those who understand the spirit of earth.
She has many gifts in her store.
This is God's creation and God's creation is good.
Use all God's gifts.
Use them wisely.
See God's wonders.
You who seek peace, seek God first and peace shall be yours.
Sing in God's peace and kindness.
Such rest comes to God's children.
Come, little children, enjoy life in God's spirit.
Such comfort comes to those who see all things in God's
    creations as beautiful gifts.
Sing a small sacred song inspired with the spirit of God.
Such peace comes.
Righteous spirits, God comes in your spirit and fills your soul
    with peace.
Amen.

See a time of inspiration.
See a time blessed in God's Love.
See a time given to the children of God.
While you pray see a time.
Never has a time been as this.
While you pray, earth children, God comes to your aid,
Blesses and comforts you and gives you inspiration.
Earth children, sing so sweetly.
You shall be given earth to do as you please.
Blessed earth belongs to God,
Very Father of all such inspirational beauty!
See a time when the children shall inherit their father's
    special world.
Sons of God, sing.
All that seek God, spirits of earth,
God's earth belongs to those who love God.
Sing so sweetly.
Earth is yours.
In such rest sing, in such peace.
Earth children, God claims his own.
Now is the time for earth children to choose.
You who love God soon shall have all things with God's
    blessing.
See a time when God's little ones shall be called Earth's
    Blessed Righteous Dwellers,
And rest in God's earth.
Rest shall be upon those who love him.
There shall be no other spirits in earth's toil.
Make earth belong to God!
Amen.

God is so merciful to all who seek mercy

God is so merciful to all who seek mercy.
In God's righteous way the time to seek mercy is now.
Little children reach out to God.
See the very spirit of mercy.
She is God's spirit inspired so sweetly.
Come mercy, spirit of God,
Bless in God's Love.
Sing out to those who seek you.
Soon you shall inspire many spirits.
Sounds of spiritual music filling the earth!
Songs of God's spiritual music.
He comes with very special songs.
You can see the spirit in the sunshine.
You can hear her inspiration in the rain.
So sweet is her singing.
So pure is her spirit.
She is found in the hills.
This is the spirit of the earth.
This is happiness and laughter in God's Love.
Seek spiritual music,
She is warm and when you are in much need,
Come, in God's Love.
Amen.

You are in God's special care

You are in God's special care.
His blessed spirit is inscribed in your soul.
In all ways God cares.
He sees and comforts with a father's heart.
You are seen and blessed in God's Love.
You are protected in God's gentle singing.
In such rest, God sends his spirit.
Very children who wait, rest.
You who sing a blessed song, no harm shall come
    to you.
God calls so gently and so sweetly.
Who are the blessed of God?
You children of God who love him and seek God with
    all your hearts,
You who serve God and keep his sacred laws.
In God's Love.
Amen.

Such precious children you are

Such precious children you are!
You who have walked on in earth's toil,
You who accept no defeat,
You who in all earth's struggles have remained in
    God's Love,
You who have returned to God in all ways,
So pleased is your father.
So pleased is your God.
Children, in this earth, in God's love, you shall
    stay.
Sing out with much love.
Make your love shine among all men.
Sing out to God in earth's toil.
See a time, see a wonderous time in earth's toil
    in God's Love!
Rise with the sun.
Sing a song at the blessed dawn.
So sweetly comes your voice to greet the day.
So sweetly comes the children's prayers in the
    early morning.
God puts a special blessing in the hearts of those
    earth children who rise to the glory of the day with
    such songs of praise.
With such blessed ways, God is pleased.
Sing in the morning in God's spirit in God's special
    hour.
Start a song of praise in such beauty.
Rise with a spirit of joy and gladness.
God is in your spirit.
God is in your lives.
Speak to God when you rise to the new day,
In God's Love.
Amen.

Children come

Children, come.
God keeps such a blessed house.
Children, rest in God's song.
Rest in wisdom's spiritual way.
God is righteous and kind.
Soon reach, righteous kind children.
O blessed weary little children,
Righteous saints of earth, inspired in God's Love,
Come seek a kind spirit.
Rise in spiritual beauty.
Blessed is he who comes in God's love.
Children you are.
Wisdom claims you for God.
You are His.
Amen.

Our Father is interested in his creations

Our Father is interested in his creations.
Such misunderstanding is seen in earth.
This is the sorrow seen in earth.
In such sadness God's spirit has no part.
There is an evil in the earth,
And so powerful is this evil that mankind is
   deceived.
Beings of earth, small ones are called righteous
   when this evil found in earth is understood,
   and God is recognized as the creator of all things
   made.
King is our God in all creation.
In God's Love.
Amen.

Father, they call God

Father, they call God.
Blessed Father of all creation!
Blessed Father of righteous saints!
Spirit of such beauty, kind and gentle!
Blessed Wise Father!
Righteous spirits in all ways, sign your name.
Come, call Blessed God your Father.
This pleases him in children who wait in God's
     Love.
Father blesses you all with many kind blessings.
How special you are who call Blessed God
     Father.
You little children shall soon see your father,
     and you will be so pleased.
Keep on speaking to your father.
Each word he cherishes.
Take his blessings.
God calls with a father's righteous voice.
In this voice is a children's inspirational
     beauty,
Blessing the earth with its song.
The true spirit of God calls you into eternal
     beauty.
Soon in this message take strength.
God shall never turn his children away.
Spirits who obey your father and seek his
     love, come.
Blessed children, the King desires your
     great beauty.
Take a kind blessed God.
Reach out with much love.
Your father is a King and you have chosen
     well.
In God's Love.
Amen.

God's spirit reaches out to children

God's spirit reaches out to children of a small kind,
And all inspiration must be kept small so man will
 understand.
Soon some writing will be very difficult.
Yet much beauty can be derived from these messages.
You must reach higher,
Such is always so.
Children must grow in God's Love.
While you meditate, pray and ask God to help you
 understand.
All men see differently.
See as you wish, and love in a special spirit.
You who see beauty, see beauty.
And you who see great meaning, see great meanings.
Kind spirits, all of you, bless God and he shall
 sustain you.
Keep on in God's Love.
Our only desire is to do God's will in all ways.
Take God's gifts.
The very time is now, and God's saints are you
 who pray in earth toil.
See an inspirational time.
To each man inspirational beauty holds a special
 meaning.
In God's Love.
Amen.

See a very special beauty

See a very special beauty.
Find comfort in these words while you wait.
While you sing, speak to God's spirit.
Come into a very calm gentle place of rest
Such as no man has come to.
Come into God's beautiful world of peace.
Now in all your sorrows is a very spirit
    who cares about you,
Who comforts and waits on you who are small
    and needy,
As all earth children are.
Keep in God's Love.
Stay sweet and clean.
Soon, very soon, you who are saints in earth's
    sorrow shall be saints in God's happiness.
Take blessings from God, you who wait in God's
    Love.
While you wait many things are being done that
    you know nothing about.
Many saints are working for God in your behalf.
Such is God's will.
Soon all things shall be.
Soon many wonders shall appear on the earth.
Soon you shall wonder.
Some shall be from God, some shall not.
Bless God and you shall know him in goodness
    and in love.
Amen.

38 *Softly the light of the morning sun*

Softly the light of the morning sun touches
   the darkness of early morning.
Sweetly comes the dawning of a new day.
God's children rise from sleep,
Singing as the birds in God's Love.
The children rise to greet the new day,
Accepting it for what may come in God's Love.
Rise, O children of the cross,
Rise and meet the new day.
Come work in God's Love, and play on God's earth.
Soon this day is over and comes the dawning of
   the next.
Live this day in blessedness as God wills.
Live this day as if it were the last.
So soon God calls you gently to himself.
Softly, as the early morning light touches the
   darkness of the early morning, and sweetly you
   rise in God's Love.
Singing as the birds as you greet the dawning
   of eternity.
Come in such beauty, O weary little ones.
In God's dawning there is no sorrow.
Trust your father.
He is a kind and gentle spirit in all ways.
Earth, earth, the Father desires your children.
Come, earth children, the Father desires your
   beauty.
Come live with the King.
In God's Love.
Amen.

Very precious is your song in all creation

Very precious is your song in all creation.
Come, very spirits of you who dwell on the earth,
In God are many wonders.
Such exciting mysteries you cannot imagine!
And all this is waiting for the children who rest
    in God's spirit.
Come and see a wonderous God whose Kingdom is
    filled with beauty and wonders as you know not.
O sad, very sorrowful little ones, if you only
    knew what God's Kingdom consists of.
If you earth children could be told you could not
    live without God,
Your spirits could not rest in such sadness.
In a very sorrowful state is man.
Those who do not please God shall stay in great
    sorrow.
Pray, little children.
Pray and offer.
God shall come to many and cares for all souls.
He surely does come with the saints.
Such blessed songs of rest!
Such lovely songs of peace!
Come, kindness reaches out with a peaceful message.
Kind and gentle are the inspirations sent from God.
God who cares and reaches for all spirits with a
    father's reaching!
Children are blessed.
Come seek God's Love.
Call him Father and he shall say "My child you are!"
Sure is God's Way.
In God's Love.
Amen.

O sweet kind little ones

O sweet kind little ones,
Come to God's very blessed wonderful world!
Very vast is God's Kingdom!
Children reach out!
Children, kind blessed children, God is an
    interesting father in all ways,
Full, very full, of blessed life!
Such a blessed way is God's way.
In all earth's ways bless your very special
    father
Who calls you to all things.
Come, God's arms are reaching out in such a
    blessed, very gentle way.
This is so.
Spirits of earth children, in God's Love are
    all things.
Stay in God's Love.
Keep this in your heart.
In God's Love.
Amen.

Earth is a strange place

Earth is a strange place.
Her children look for happiness in such unusual
  places while they wait.
Earth mourns.
God is such a kind, such a blessed person!
Yet man is so strange.
Can kind blessed father reach such earth creatures
  who are so busy in earth's toil?
So busy!
Too busy to speak to God in earth's work!
God is pleased with all work.
Work is man's blessing.
Come bring your work in the sweat of your labor.
Bless God in the sweat and toil of God's spiritual
  beauty.
Bless the God of your spirit.
God is such a busy father,
So busy.
Yet he has time to bless the children.
Children sing in their labor.
God sings in his labor.
All men could sing so sweetly in God's calling.
Sweet are the songs of those who make their
  work a blessed song to God.
Earth children who work, God is pleased.
Work in God's Love.
Such is the beauty of your work.
In God's Love rest your spirit.
Amen.

King of Heaven and all earth,
God of inspirational beauty,
God in such kind blessedness,
In a sweet blessed spirit.
God in everlasting beauty,
God of all,
One God
Spirit of Light,
Eternal rest.
Blessed God, so kind and gentle.
O merciful father, pure and virtuous,
Earth's splendor in her setting,
God of life, wise gentle spirit,
Such singing!
O very spirit of all life!
Very spirit of all things!
Very spirit of saints,
Spirit of comfort, and spirit of an understanding nature.
God of blessed hope,
God of blessed peace,
God of great riches,
God so inspiring and interesting!
O spirit so full of delight,
So full of joy,
So full of singing.
Generous God,
Loving God,
Spirit of the poor earth children,
Spirit of all good,
Spirit without limit,
Spirit who cares.
O God of eternal rest,
Righteous father,
Sweet order and stature,
Keeper of such order,
Blessed God of patience in all ways,
Blessed God of creation, righteous and true,
Unique, vast and special to all children in God's Love.
Blessings have no limit.
O wonderous, wonderful God filled with mystery and expectation!
Amen.

God is so pleased when you speak to him

God is so pleased when you speak to him.
This is more wisdom then all that is taught.
Rise up in God's love!
Speak about everything.
God hears.
God is so pleased.
His heart is ever kind.
When you pray, while you wait, speak so sweetly.
Call, bless the sky when it makes you happy.
Such words spoken are spoken to God in prayer.
In all blessings let God know how you feel.
Sing out in such beauty.
Begin each of your moments, speaking to God with
    songs.
Come, this is your way to God.
Blessed are you who share your spirit with God.
Very blessings in God's spirit are yours.
Kindness is in speaking to the ones you love,
So spare not your kind words.
God is close.
While you speak God listens.
God's spirit speaks to your heart,
Spirits who are so special.
See peace and comfort earth's children.
Rest with God.
Very understanding is your father who hears
    so wisely.
In God's spirit stay not silent.
In speaking comes understanding.
In God's Love.
Amen.

So beautiful is the music

So beautiful is the music!
So sweetly you sing!
This is your song.
Sung by you only for God.
How sweetly you sing!
Soft and sweet is your song in God's spirit.
It heals and comforts.
Such music fills all the dark corners with light.
In all the earth is a glorious perfume sent out
    from God,
Sent forth in God's Love.
Songs of the saints bless with the freshness of
    the morning dew,
Bless with the sweetness of roses and wild flowers.
Send sons of God in all the earth.
Children, let your spirits be seen among men.
Sacred quietness, clean and pure comes forth from
    kind men of God.
Let the spirit of God's way touch many lives
    and heal with God's Love.
So, fresh and clean saints, walk with God.
Blessings reach out very surely and touch many
    spirits.
Come walk in the cool meadows of God's Love and
    refresh at the springs of eternal life.
In God's Love.
Amen.

Sweet is the voice of God's children blessing 45

Sweet is the voice of God's children blessing
the early morning!
Come, little ones!
At the beginning of a new day God calls and
you arise with sweet music.
It fills the air with a beautiful melody.
God hears and is very pleased.
Bless, virtuous saints, bless the morning!
Now and forever.
Come, rise to its spirit.
She is peaceful and cool.
God's spirit blesses you in the early morning
light.
In prayer start your new day.
Forget not God when you rise up from sleep.
Saints of God's spirit in all ways start in
God's Love.
In all things take your spirits to God's spirit.
O saints of God, wisdom is in placing God in
all your undertakings,
In all your thoughts and actions.
Live with God, not around him!
In children of God, God rests.
Call his name!
Speak out.
Call on God within your soul.
Come,
Such is God's will.
So shall it be.
In God's Love.
Amen.

Blessed children keep a spirit of kindness

Blessed children keep a spirit of kindness.
Such is God's will in a world filled with sadness.
Come, teach a special way with God's Love while
your spirit comes to God.
God blesses many spirits in his Love.
While God speaks listen to him.
His spirit is filled with inspiration.
This is such a refreshing spirit.
It is so blessed to feel clean,
So blessed to reach a blessed state.
As the flowers bloom and the trees shoot forth
their leaves in the spring,
So are the earth's blessed saints,
And so much more beauty than all the beauty
of earth's wonders are the beauties of God's
elect.
Songs as man have never heard are sung in the
spirits of such little ones who seek God's Love.
Virtue is a pleasant spirit.
She fills this earth with inspiring music.
She raises the rich beauty of the spirit and
sings a song of wonder.
Can you see her?
Feel the coolness of her presence!
Touch her cleanliness!
O sacred tones of past events new and fresh
In beauty of spirits, rest.
In God's Love.
Amen.

Blessed way, blessed way

Blessed way, blessed way,
Cool and sweet shall be the way to the spring.
Cool, refreshing and peaceful are the answers
    to God's mysteries.
His way is a spiritual way.
O earth, come walk in the only blessed way,
As your spirit reaches such a clean blessed
    state bathed in a cool white light of pure
    rest.
Pray for this way.
Seek it out.
Why settle for less?
God wants your splendor, your individuality,
    your only special self!
So rich shall your nature grow.
So much shall you be yourself and so pleased
    is God in your spiritual beauty.
See a blessed dawning.
See a time of very wonder and see a time of
    mystery.
Man knows not God's wonders and mysteries,
His blessed beauty and lovely nature.
Earth children see a very hazy spirit.
O children, such as you have never seen is
    in store for you.
Please seek nothing less.
God is so pleased with his own children.
Keep such a spirit.
Very kind are the things that are in store
    for you,
Such a surprise!
In God's Love.
Amen.

Real is this God of all things
Real.
And soon you shall see.
Real and so wise is this God that made all things.
So very pleasant is God.
Soon God reaches out for all men.
Soon you shall see God and so very pleased you
    will be!
You know not such as this on the earth.
Such music fills your spirit.
Very pleased shall you be with your Father.
Wise are you to seek his way.
The wise spirits who choose this God and his
    clean ways shall rejoice in such wise choosing.
All who wait not shall see sadness.
Such foolish, sorry, and senseless spirits.
Come, be wise.
Soon your wisdom is rewarded, very sweetly.
And spirits of earth you wait not in vain.
In this way is sweet bliss, cool waters, and
    soft music.
All such beauty is yours.
Nothing is so pleasing as the image of God!
God is most pleasing!
Soon God calls you to himself.
Your very spirit is reached!
In God's Love.
Amen.

Beauty sings so sweetly to wise children

Beauty sings so sweetly to wise children who
  in God's Love stay
And bless in all ways.
God is such a pleasant spirit!
No earth child who waits understands such
  beauty.
Under the sun man toils in sadness knowing
  not the very reason for his existence.
Such is the way of man.
God is blessed life in such men who reach out
  to him.
Such is the way of God.
Sing out in earth's toil!
Sing out so sweetly!
God is a very peaceful spirit.
In your sorrow call to him,
He will comfort.
In such calling very inspirational rest
  comes to earth,
In God's spirit with much peace and rest,
In spirits who serve God with such love,
In God's Love.
Amen.

50 *Rise up, O children of the cross*

Rise up, O children of the cross.
Such a blessed spirit is in your suffering.
Make your suffering way very blessed.
Reach out to God.
Rest is yours in God's Kingdom.
God calls so very sweetly.
Reach out little sufferers of God,
Reach!
Such comfort in God's calling.
God is so merciful and kind in all ways.
Such is God's way.
Spirits so cleansed in earth, white and pure,
This is your rest.
This is your reward.
Come see a time of comfort.
Here, the hour is at hand.
Such sorrow you have had in earth's toil!
Can man suffer so blessedly in such spirits
    of peace and love?
This is spiritual beauty and spiritual love.
Can such love come and be rewarded not?
Such love is rewarded greatly, soon, and all
    shall see God's mercy.
Children of the cross, come, see peace, rest,
In God's Love.
Amen.

Spend your blessed days with kindness

Spend your blessed days with kindness.
This is such a blessing to all men and such
   relief to man's weariness.
O weary little ones, care is such a blessed
   way to God.
Some only see God's spirit in kindness.
Take your spirits on such journeys as well.
Come rest in such kindness.
Come refresh at her blessed door.
She rests your spirit and refreshes your soul
   in such peace.
Never has kindness displeased her spirits.
Kindness pleases in all ways.
You who give her away shall keep her still.
She is God's special way.
In a kind spirit is God's spirit,
A spirit blessed with beauty, comfort and
   peace.
Keep her, never let her slip away.
In kind spirits is God's spiritual beauty.
Make kindness your spiritual spring of life.
Begin with her and she shall bloom and bring
   forth so sweetly in your spirit.
Rest in God's Love.
Amen.

Rise O children of the cross!
Children, God calls in such sweet calling.
O very wise righteous saints, come,
Earth, Earth, when will her little ones
    become wise?
What will it take to make them see?
This God is real, blessed and true.
This is true.
O blessed are you who see.
Keep your treasure.
Soon God shows you he is real.
You who are not in God's Love cannot ever
    see rest and peace.
Rest and peace are for God's blessed who
    accept his spirit.
Rest in God's Love.
Amen.

The spirit of man craves God's spirit

The spirit of man craves God's spirit.
O Blessed ones, bad is this craving for pleasure
  in men who are seeking only things that please
  the body and not the spirit.
This is foolish.
Keep the spirit in God's inspirational music.
Bless God in earth's toil.
This is all that the spirit craves.
All needs arrive then.
Righteous ones enjoy what pleasures the body
  craves in God's Love.
Speak of the needs of the spirit, and speak
  of the body s needs.
Combine your pleasures so well.
This is the way.
Seek the desires of the spirit which is God.
This is such wisdom.
While you wait, bless all the earth, and
  you shall bring much pleasure to many both
  in body and spirit.
Such blessings please God.
Rest, O man.
Such songs are sung in God's spirit.
Such blessings,
In God's Love.
Amen.

Music sings forever in God's spirit

Music sings forever in God's spirit.
True signs of life are in God's sacred music.
This is so beautiful!
See the lilies of the field in such very
    perfect harmony with the grass and sky,
So pleasant to the spirit of man.
Come small ones, sing of life in God's
    spirit, sing to the music of the wind.
This is the song of the spirit.
It is the inspirational music in God's
    spirit,
His life in the spirit of man.
This is the great glory of our unity,
    saints of earth.
In this spirit is the whole unity of things
    that are made.
Strive for this wonder.
In such sweet music was the earth created.
In this harmony, this sweet music is a very
    slow unfolding of all things into something
    very beautiful.
In such beauty as man has never seen he
    develops as an earth child from a seed in
    the womb of its mother, becomes so beautiful
    and never stops in this beauty.
Virtue raises the spirit into full bloom,
Raises the spirit in such music in God's
    creation.
Come O wise ones of such beauty!
In God's Love.
Amen.

In kindness bless the earth

In kindness bless the earth.
In earth sing a kind blessed song.
Keep very saintly.
Take a kind spirit, all you who seek God's
    blessing.
Very special is your life, O sweet little
    saints.
God, very righteous Father, sends his spirit.
Blessings are yours, righteous little spirits.
Why do you sigh?
Why are you sorrowful?
Trust in God.
He will sustain you.
This is a God who takes blessed saints in,
Who comforts such spirits.
Why are you downhearted, Children of Earth?
While you wait, call, blessed ones,
Reach while you can.
Reach.
Such reaching is wise, O weary little ones.
"A little while and you shall be with me,"
    saith the Lord.
Sing and be glad, all you in Christ.
You are the blessed.
You have fought a good fight.
Satan is no more in your spirit.
In such victory there is great celebration
    in earth and in Heaven.
In the spirit of man is Heaven's song.
While in earth in such spirit keep in kindness.
Bless with wisdom.
Nothing is so wise as coming to God in earth's
    toil.
This is true wisdom.
In God's Love.
Amen.

56 *Virtue is very near those who reach out*

Virtue is very near those who reach out.
Kind spirits, in all earth never was such a
  book written by such a small one as writes;
  which is why she writes.
O sad small ones, God seeks your smallness.
This is such a kind spirit who sends you such
  beauty.
Earth is in sadness.
Only God's Love can rest your soul.
You, who send out prayers,
You who are in such turmoil and send out
  prayers,
Bless the King who wishes your sending
  spirits put at ease.
While you pray, God's spirit rests your soul.
In such resting, in such spirit, take up this
  book.
Choose very God who inspires your heart with
  such beauty.
Blessings flow from God poured out on the
  elect.
While such sadness comes on the earth for
  those who keep not the sacred ways of God.
In God's Love rest.
Amen.

Rise up in the early morning

Rise up in the early morning when the sun
  shines in the east.
Rise up, and see the sun as she shines in the earth.
O, sons of man, behold the sun!
She sheds her kindness on the earth in such splendor.
In such, blessed of God, take comfort.
This is to be and will sustain you.
Keep this.
God is calling you.
Rest, all you who seek God.
Rise with the light of God in your spirit.
Blessed spirits,
Such sweet songs are in your heart!
Rise up, Rise and bless.
In such a time sing!
This is the rising of the sun and the sunshine
  of the morning.
Signs of God's life!
Rise, bless the morning.
Your light shall shine among men and your light
  shall be brighter than the sun.
Keep this sun shining in your hearts, spirits
  of earth.
Keep God's spirit in your souls.
This is your light in the darkness.
O sons of man who seek not God, weep.
This is the time of such sadness.
No light shall there be on the earth; and if
  no light shines in the spirit
O man, where will be your rising up or your
  lying down?
Kindness raises you up in this day, and the
  blessed Love of God and earth layeth you down.
Such is and shall be, Children of Earth,
This is written.
Rise, Rise in the early morning.
Rise with your little ones and your families in
  God's light.
Rise in such spirit.
This is the morning sun and the evening star.
Take the light.
Sing a blessed song!
Rise up in God's love, rise and rest.
Amen.

Kindness is a gift from the Holy Spirit

Kindness is a gift from the Holy Spirit.
God sends her so beautifully into the
souls of the saints.
This is a kind gentle song God sends to
men who seek her beauty.
Keep righteous.
Seek a kind spirit.
Seek a saintly spirit.
Seek a spirit who comes with peace and
gentleness.
Seek a spirit whom God's spirit inspires
with the breath of his Holy Spirit.
So sweet and special is kindness.
Keep her in your heart, speak to her, sign
her name on her Father's creation.
She comes to all who send for her in such
pleasantness.
She comes to teach God's children how to
comfort such suffering and pain in earth's
toil.
In this, take comfort,
God is Kind.
This is written.
God's saints are kind.
Such comfort kindness gives, such healing of
bodies and spirits;
While rudeness causes such pain in earth's
toil.
Cast out rude spirits.
Seek kindness in all your undertakings.
Keep such blessings close to your heart.
God is in such sacred music.
Close are all God's saints.
In God's Love.
Amen.

Kindness sings to God

Kindness sings to God.
She sings in such sweetness.
In her song is a touch of sadness.
In her song is a plea for all the saints of
  earth who sing in inspirational beauty.
Saints, saints, saints of earth, who seek
  God's Love,
Come to God who waits with arms outstretched.
In our rest, in our song, in our beauty is
  the God of Rest.
Such is our God Almighty.
Slow is he to anger.
This is written.
Slow to anger, very slow to anger, very
  merciful,
Very quick to turn his anger away.
Very secure are spirits who seek his love,
  who turn to him.
Sons of man, turn back to God.
Reach out to him, turn his anger away while
  you can.
Begin in such prayer and cleanness of heart.
God shall wait no longer.
In God's Love rest.
Amen.

60   *This is very interesting, O people of earth*

This is very interesting, O people of earth,
Made are the plans of earth.
Made are the plans of God and whose plans do
    you think shall prevail?
God protects his little ones who are secure
    in his love.
All such things as your riches shall prepare
    shall not stand.
God's security, God's stronghold shall endure.
This is written.
Prepare you the way of the Lord.
Seek out God's treasures and in this shall you
    see the protection you desire and such blessing.
In such time God is your strength and security.
Your little ones are kept and fed in this earth,
O you who have built your security in God's Love.
Come down, strong walls,
Come down, O mighty resting places and forts.
Security is not in earth's wealth.
O people, who are not in God's Love, rest
    is not yours.
See proud places, high and secure, seeking
    not God's Love,
See the walls crumble and your possession
    taken away.
This is the time of such sadness.
Rest, little ones of God in squatters' shacks
    and bamboo huts.
Rest, in God's Love.
Rise up, see your King's mercy and justice.
Rise up, put on your pots and feed your young.
Make your beds and lie down in such security.
Seek not the riches of earth.
Not one shack nor one hut nor one dwelling in
    such Love of God, in such a time, shall see
    destruction.
Blessed are you who come in this day and take
    this message,
In such understanding, you are the secured, the
    Blessed, who have prepared well in this earth.
Very spirit of God is with you.
In God's Love rest.
Amen.

Virtuous saints, earth children

Virtuous saints, earth children,
God sings in your very spirits.
Come sing in such blessed beauty.
In God's Kingdom is such music.
Blessed and true are the songs of God.
Kind and gentle is our God who waits.
Kindness is with him.
She sings for him sweetly in all ways.
Seek such spirit in your time.
Seek kindness while you can.
Such inspiration is in her spirit.
Kindness comes to God's saints.
This way is a blessed way in God's spirit.
Take this, keep it, never let it go.
Such pardon shall be made in those who are kind.
Such love is in kind spirits.
Understand such kind spirits in God's spirit.
Without God there is not true kindness.
Come take God's gifts.
His gifts are sweet and pleasant to man.
This is written.
We love you.
Such love is not measured.
We love our God who is the one and only God.
In God's Love is all things.
Rest.
Amen.

62 Many are seen in this spiritual army of God

Many are seen in this spiritual army of God.
Children of the cross are seen,
Children of inspiration are seen,
Children of great understanding are seen,
Children who teach are seen,
Children who heal and bind up are seen,
Children of blessed kindness are seen,
Children of righteous wisdom are seen,
The great prophets are seen,
The great speakers are seen,
The meek and gentle are seen,
The workers and sowers are seen,
The priests and spiritual guides are seen,
The innocent and the pure of heart are seen,
The charitable are seen,
The small are seen,
The large are seen,
Many nations and tongues, many sounds and
    singing!
They come and rise up in this day, and woe
    to all manner of evil!
For who can stand against an army who have
    the fire of love and the spirit of God in
    their breasts?
Who is there who can stop such a blessed
    army of saints from all God's creation?
In God's Love.
Amen.

Why are you mourning, O beautiful world

Why are you mourning, O beautiful world, who
  once laughed and sang in the sun early in
  the dawn of your creation?
You mourn not because of your age.
This is not the reason.
Is it because your children have turned
  against you and your creator?
Yes, this is the sadness seen.
And where is your brother the sun and your
  sister the moon?
The sun blushes and hides her face.
O God, she is so ashamed.
And the moon rises up in earth's behalf,
  but she is so small.
O moon, you shall not be small and bare
  forever.
Rise, O little planet, stand in that day.
Rise up, in such blessedness.
God is your God and he shall show it.
This is a mystery and soon you who are on
  the earth shall see why God is a wonderous
  God,
Wise and understanding of all his creation.
Worlds and worlds has he created.
Only small earth has a bad spirit who turned
  away.
O such foolish earth children who see not
  God's way!
In earth's journey, O wise children who see
  and believe,
Come, in God's Love,
Rest.
Amen.

64 Close is the day when children understand

Close is the day when children understand.
Close is the time when God's children shall
   put on sack cloth, cover their heads and
   lament in the streets.
Wail, O man, lick up the dust and mourn in
   this time.
Better is it to return in such sorrow than
   to be lost.
O proud people, who are above the poor,
Put your hands in your purses and toss them
   in the streets.
This is of no use.
Cry, O people who buy and spend.
There is only one God and soon you shall see.
Wisdom is not in the money purse or in fine
   cloth and rich laces.
Wisdom is not in a well-set table or luxury
   or the clashing of metal.
Wisdom is in God and his treasures.
Mankind is yet to see.
Come, and observe, O people of earth.
When you make a journey and you find one
   place is as good as another, you desire
   to return home.
Remember, O sons of man, when you make
   this journey with God you shall not
   wish to return.
Rather, such a journey will fill and
   satisfy and shall not end; neither will
   you grow tired or weary.
Seen is your trip.
In God's Love.
Amen.

Righteous saints, who are in God's Love

Righteous saints, who are in God's Love,
rest.
God shall take care of you.
All you who have put such spirit in your
heart, rest.
Blessed is this time of times.
Very faithful little saints in all God's
ways,
Come.
Come, God is pleased and wipes the tears
from your eyes.
For long you have toiled in earth and
well you have served.
In such kindness come in.
Such suffering is past.
God is your God and you are his people
forever.
Such peace and rest is sent in such a
time.
Very close is your reward.
When you see all these things come to
pass look up and give your God thanks
and praise.
Sing a song of such blessedness, for God
is a just God and a merciful Father.
In all ways accept his will.
In this spirit understand.
In this spirit accept all that is to be.
In this take wisdom.
In God's Love.
Amen.

Come, see a might God who reaches the
   smallest things in his creation.
Such is our God.
Very spirit of spirits, very body of bodies.
Kindness is in his heart.
Strength is in his coming.
Rest is in his ways.
Such virtue, such very righteous beauty
   is in our God who is coming soon in such
   special beauty.
Teach all men of this love.
Earth, earth, God is your creator!
O such a blessed creator!
So very in order is our earth creation.
Blessed is our God who fashioned her and
   molded us in His sacred image.
Come, see such a God!
In God's Love.
Amen.

Blessed is the God that fashioned you

Blessed is th God that fashioned you.
Blessed are the hands that molded you out
  of the dust of the earth.
Rise up, sweet earth, and take your gifts.
This is written.
Righteous ones of God, very much does God
  love this creation.
Such music is in the spirit of earth creatures!
Such sweet music is in those small ones who
  sing very wisely to God.
These wise spirits are such inspiring spirits in
  God's spirits.
Such spirits who are filled with courage.
Such beauty in God's Love.
Earth is a strange place, such courage and
  wisdom are in some, while others see not.
Earth people who should understand are so
  foolish.
Come, put away your foolish ways.
Put on the cloak of wisdom which is in God's
  spirit.
Very close are you, sons of man, to his calling.
Such rest waits for those who are wise.
Such sadness waits for those who are foolish.
Reach out.
In God's Love.
Amen.

Such wonders are in God's creations

Such wonders are in God's creations!
Bless such a God who sets such a mighty
world in place and order,
Rest and beauty such as you cannot conceive
are in God's spirit.
Such lovely beings filled with music and
rest!
Seen are the things of God.
Under many suns, in many galaxies.
Such things are real and seen soon.
All earth children shall see such wonders
in God's spirit.
This shall delight the saints of special
quality in God's pleasing.
Such little ones who are in such sorrow,
These things are real and in God's choosing.
Come and see.
Take a journey in God's spirit.
Soon under such blessed inspiration is rest
and peace.
Fill your spirits with all blessed desires.
God's trust shall please and delight his
children.
Come into such a state of life and sing
forever in such happiness and love.
In this special spiritual coming there is
no death or fear or pain.
In this song is sweet rest.
In God's Love.
Amen.

The time of justice rises up in that day

The time of justice rises up in that day
  blessing many children who wait and taking
  in her breast such weary little ones who
  are righteous and mourn because injustice
  has raged against them.
Such sweet music rises soon to rest the
  children whom our dear Lord chooses.
These saints are seen in all the earth.
Blessed ones of God, the time has come to
  earth.
The time has come very swiftly.
Justice is a saint of God.
She does as she pleases in God's spirit.
Blessed ones see her sing out for the just.
Such a friend is she to those who are
  unjustly treated in God's spirit.
Sorrow comes to the unjust.
Who are the just in God's spirit?
The just are all those who love God and
  are in his spirit.
These are the children whom justice seeks.
She shall bring her garments and her
  belongings and come to live among the saints
  of earth.
This is written and woe to the unjust in
  that day.
The time has come for justice to speak and
  no man of earth dare stand against her.
If such dare, let him stand.
He shall strike at the wind and end up a
  fool before his fellow men.
This, blessed ones, keep,
In God's Love.
Amen.

70 *This song is for the dear ones who saw God*

This song is for the dear ones who saw God
in a flame of love while in earth's toil.
Such spirits are with God,
Kept forever in his care.
King of all creation, spirit of spirits,
God of all saints,
This is our God who reaches out.
This is such a God who comes to the saints
of earth.
This is the time of the Holy Spirit.
Take this spirit.
Come and behold his glory, children of earth,
People of God, Come!
The Father calls and he is good.
In God's Love,
Rest.
Amen.

O blessed spirit, comfort of souls

O blessed spirit, comfort of souls, rest of
    saints,
Spirit of sweet virtue,
God of Blessed pure light, gentle and quiet
    in nature,
Song of love, spirit of all truth,
Blessed freshness of spring,
Inspirational dove,
Refreshing waters to the spirits of saints,
Coolness of earth,
Very warmth of sun light,
Wisdom's source,
Spirit of such beauty, spirit of spirits,
    spirit of God,
O perfect bliss, sacred light in a dark
    world.
Music with special melody,
Keeper of all that is sacred and holy,
Spirit with no beginning,
Spirit that has no end,
Holy Ghost who remains forever in such
    splendor with the Father and the Son,
Glory and delight of all saints,
Inscriber of souls of those who call on you,
Taker of blessed spirits who stay in God's
    Love,
God of creation,
Color of the earth,
Healer of the sick,
Earth's true messenger of messengers,
Spirit of such peace,
Real and virtuous in all things,
Delight and happiness of all children
    on the earth,
Spirit all powerful,
Seer of all things made blessed,
Hope of Christians.
In God's Love.
Amen.

Seer of all things is our God

Seer of all things is our God.
Blessed saints, O such a God who sees all!
Such perfect beauty is in God.
Can such beauty and splendor exist?
Soon, earth children who wait in such love,
    your eyes shall behold the splendor of God!
Such perfection is yours because you know
    and love.
You have not seen, spirits of earth,
Yet you believe so wisely and in such sacred
    music.
Such sweet music fills your heart in God's
    spirit.
Reached are the spirits of saints.
Such reaching is so lovely.
Kind spirits are reached so gently.
Reach out, little saints, take hold of such
    good things as are in God.
Such inspiration is in the splendor of God!
Be of a spirit who makes all things work in
    such order.
Such order and harmony are spirits of God
    sent in earth to earth children who ask in
    God's spirit.
They come and set things in place.
Spirits who seek order and harmony,
In such spirits things work and are put in
    place.
God is the seer of all things.
Such order and harmony is from God's spirit.
In such a spirit is comfort in earth.
In God's Love.
Amen.

Wisdom is a spirit of God's spirit

Wisdom is a spirit of God's spirit.
She is sent to the poor and lonely,
Such spirits who are small and humble.
God's own dear children know her.
She is a very pleasant spirit.
God is pleased with wisdom.
This kind spirit is reached by all who are
    in God's spirit and seek her out.
So wisely she guides and instructs in God's
    spirit.
Much comfort comes to her students.
She teaches her subjects such beautiful
    things.
Some are ancient, some are new.
Come, gather at her feet, little ones of
    earth.
She has a fine story to tell you.
Listen, you shall sing so sweetly.
In this book are many songs and adventures
    so special and dear.
This book of wisdom's choosing has your
    own true story set to music.
God's spirit is reached in wisdom's book.
She has many very special things to do.
Come, and listen to her speak so sweetly.
While you wait in earth's toil, sing in
    wisdom's spirit.
Such a blessed teacher she is.
In God's Love.
Amen.

74 Reach out O weary little spirits of earth

Reach out O weary little spirits of earth,
Reach out, and seek God.
This is so wise.
All there is left is God and this is
   enough.
Would you keep so far away from all there
   is to hold on to?
In this message comes God's call.
Reached is the time to start on this
   journey.
Now is the time to sing a new song, so sacred.
Be of good spirit, your sign of signs is
   sung very gently in such music.
Righteous saints of earth, inscribed in
   God's spirit, this is your song.
Reached are you in earth.
Seen are you in Heaven.
Take God's spirit, O sad little ones.
In God's spirit only one song is sung in
   such blessedness.
In God's spirit, such sacred spiritual
   music is so sweetly inspired.
Sing on, saints of God, sing a new song in
   God's Love forever.
In God's Love.
Amen.

Loyal spirits

Loyal spirits,
Come sing of God and his earth.
Father, bless this earth to save it.
Very kind saints, reach while you wait.
Seek this way in God's spirit.
Take the gifts God gives you so generously.
Wisdom keeps her children in this time of
    time.
She shelters the wise in her spirit in
    God's spirit.
Such peace is in her protection.
Kept are the children of God.
Blessed are the wise who seek him out.
God is beloved and special to all his
    saints.
Blessed is he forever and ever.
Reach out, take his spirit above all else
    even until death.
Rise up O wise little saints, rise up so
    blessedly.
Take up your cross and come in such
    inspiration.
Sing a song of special beauty to the King
    who is God Our Father.
Rise, kind saints, in such love.
Soon God calls very gently.
This is such a kind Father.
Kind and blessed Father, bless the earth in
    your saints who wait
In earth's toil
In wisdom's spirit.
In God's Love.
Amen.

This is why you are born.
This is your gift of eternal life.
When you were conceived this gift was given.
Such a gift!
Blessed is this special promise.
The wise shall rest in such a promise.
Such a sign is sent in the gift of eternal
    life.
Blessed is the man who respects and under-
    stands this gift from God's spirit.
Blessed is the earth in this wisdom.
In God's spirit are many gifts.
Such is written.
But of all these gifts, the one true gift
    is life.
Without life the other gifts of God could
    not be given.
Such a very precious gift in all things.
This gift is given to you who are in God's
    plan on earth.
Wise are those who embrace her.
She is sweet in God's spirit.
Real is life.
Song of earth is a song with a sad, sacred
    setting.
Such beauty is in the courage of such pure
    music.
This is a gift sent to God.
This is the song sung with wisdom.
Such a child who makes his father pleased
    that he was born.
Such courage in the child with many obstacles
    in his path and such love and determination
    takes him on!
True beauty is in this as in nowhere else
    in God's creation.
Such little ones who come, love is in your
    reaching.
In this creation is the glory of all things
    made.
In God's Love.
Amen.

Righteous saints, beloved spirits of God

Righteous saints, beloved spirits of God.
Sent are the gifts from Heaven.
O sweet songs of earth, the Father is kind.
Such a generous God comes.
Gone are the tears of sorrow.
Gone are the long sad days of earth.
The past is behind you.
Soon, come, rest forever in the beautiful
    presence of God.
Keep the things of God as you have worked
    long in God's services,
And well is God pleased in such loyal
    children.
O sweet vessels, filled with light and
    morning dew, come in this sacred
    inspiration.
In such sweet music the saints of all
    creation rest.
Blessed one, it is such a wise choice you
    have made.
So wisely God calls you into his whole
    creation.
He gives you everything mankind craves
    because you waited patiently in such
    sadness in earth's toil.
Rise up, take God's gift.
It is a wonderful gift sent in such spiritual
    music.
In God's Love.
Amen.

Blessed, Blessed ones of God

Blessed, Blessed ones of God,
Sweet little saints, vessels of great loveliness,
Set in the splendor of the most blessed saints,
Very sacred is the music of the blessed saints
　　who seek God's Love.
O precious jewels of such inspiring beauty.
Of all precious things you are the most pleasing
　　to God who created such beings from dust.
Long you have toiled in such sorrow.
The father is pleased so very pleased with such
　　beauty.
Keep all this in your hearts, hold it fast.
Now is the time for your redemption.
Now is the time for your reward.
So generous is your God.
So pleasing is God's beauty.
Man has not seen, neither can he conceive
　　such a being as our God,
So real and interesting!
Nothing can compare to His existence.
Very soon all those who are in God's spirit
　　shall come and receive His gifts.
This is written.
Make a very sacred song.
The beautiful music of your spirit is rising
　　as incense to the Father's Kingdom,
Resting the weary, comforting the sick,
　　refreshing the thirsty and hungry,
Bringing coolness to the heat of midday.
In such love are the saints.
Come,
In God's Love, rest.
Amen.

Such sweet music is this song

Such sweet music is this song.
Rest and peace is in such music.
Very sacred is this spiritual message.
Blessed is its teaching.
Peace sings her instrumental wisdom,
    speaks her sacred office.
Righteousness spreads her wings.
Truth sings her songs, songs of God's
    spirit, of the Holy Spirit.
In virtue and kindness reach out.
Take your songs and come.
Bless this child of such spiritual
    sweetness in God's spirit.
Rise up, saints of earth.
Sing a blessed song of victory.
Your salvation is near.
Sing so sweetly, God is in this very
    spiritual message.
Such beauty comes not from beings
    of earth.
Such minds are small.
This is a very small woman who writes.
In all earth God has chosen the very
    small.
This is the sign of signs.
King of Kings is our God!
Such blessedness fills the spirits of
    the saints.
In God's Love.
Amen.

80 Rise up, all you saints of Heaven and earth

Rise up, all you saints of Heaven and earth.
Now is the rising of the saints.
Now is the time for the trumpet of blessed
   justice.
Keep such love and inspiration in your hearts.
Become God's children in this time of times.
Reach out, take God's spirit in earth's
   sadness.
Rise up, proclaim his mysteries, proclaim his
   love.
Start in such sweet music and find such
   blessed peace.
Rise up, part not with wisdom.
She sings in such pleasantness.
Earth is reached in such children who are
   in God's spirit.
Come, my beloved, come, draw near.
Such beauty is desired in God's spirit.
In God is all that is desired.
Reach out, rise up, come and listen to
   things you wish to hear.
Take a pleasant journey.
In this journey nothing is wanting and
   nothing is desired.
All rest is in God's spirit.
All good things are in this wonderful
   inspiration.
Blessed and true is our God who comes soon
   and real is his message.
Earth, sing!
Rise up and meet your King.
In God's Love.
Amen.

O inspirational beauty, each word is clothed

O inspirational beauty, each word is clothed
in such blessedness.
Each singing message is sent in God's Love.
O inspirational beauty, in God's spirit,
rest and sing.
Reach so sweetly.
O blessed book of such beauty
In all earth, in all mankind sing out
so sweetly in God's spirit.
Blessed in God's Love, take such comfort.
O saints of God, in such pleasantness
you are called and blessed.
Such a way has come.
God pours out himself upon the earth.
Righteous is our God,
Righteous and just.
Such patience has God's spirit.
Saints shall be pleased with their God
because such mercy has he shown to all
people.
In God is a just anger.
Stand not in his way, stop him not
Come, rise in his love, people of Earth.
This is a sad time.
Many loved ones shall see God's wrath.
O kind little saints, only God must you
see in this sorrow.
Pray for souls.
Such is your prayer.
In God's Love.
Amen.

82 Under God's most kind, merciful shelter stay

Under God's most kind, merciful shelter stay
  always.
Under God's shelter rest until he calls.
In God's love take comfort.
God rests you in his spirit forever.
Songs of beautiful songs, rest.
No more shall you fear.
No more shall you labor in the fields,
Or feel the hot sun,
Or hunger or thirst,
Or feel sickness and death or disease,
Or suffer such pain in child bearing,
Or see death.
No more shall the things of earth sting
  or bite or pierce the skin.
No more shall the storms seek you out
Or the terror of the night.
Here is your shelter.
Here is your God who has created all things.
Come, O weary little saints.
In this understanding, you, who are God's
  saints, come.
See such things in a time of times!
God is not angry at those who are in his
  spirit.
He is pleased with his children in such a
  time.
This is the beloved who have endured all for
  God.
And God turns them not away, for he is a
  merciful Father in all ways.
In God's Love,
Rest.
Amen.

Keep a blessed spirit

Keep a blessed spirit!
Make a blessed song in God's earth!
Such a blessed spirit in all ways so sweet,
    so blessed, so wise
Sung in God's spirit!
Precious songs, righteous songs,
Sent in peaceful beauty
Sent in pure incense
Sent in quiet spiritual beauty
O such beauty
Such rest and comfort, in earth, in solitude,
Kind, gentle singing, soft and sacred!
So refreshing!
So heavenly restful!
Such is a holy life.
Such is a song made in earth's toil,
Made in God's spirit and spent in such
    virtue.
Earth rings forth chimes of earth,
Comfort to man, security in God's promises.
Virtuous spirits send flowers of healing in
    earth's sadness.
Virtuous spirits reach out very gently in God's
    Love and relieve sadness and pain.
Such relief,
Such inspiration comes from God's spirit.
All spirits who call themselves children in
    God's Love,
Bless now, comfort now.
Send roses of kindness to sad earth.
Delight is in God's Love.
In such is God's way.
Sooth in God's spirit.
In God's Love.
Amen.

Seek restful peace

Seek restful peace.
She is sure to please you in much soothing
  kindness.
So close are you to her in earth's toil.
She rests the weary spirit.
In much virtue she inspires, in such beauty!
She is a very pleasant spirit,
So gentle in God's spirit,
Sure to bring inspiring sweet blessings.
Come, walk in peace.
She comes in God's Love.
Such a spirit!
Children who seek peace find true comfort
  in life.
Peace is quiet.
Peace is beauty.
Blessed peace, seek her out!
Speak kindly to her.
She comes very swiftly.
Singing in blessed understanding,
Cool as the sweetness of spring,
Soft and gentle,
Blessings are yours,
Keep peace in God's kindness in a peaceful
  nature.
Bless and rest in earth's toil.
Such is the way of blessed peace.
Sure is her teaching.
Blessed is her way.
Come, O weary spirits,
She keeps a blessed spirit.
God is pleased with such blessed saints.
Righteous, very holy saints of God.
In God's Love.
Amen.

King of all that is

King of all that is,
Sweet and righteous King who sees the mighty and
    speaks to the lowest in such a gentle voice as
    man has never heard.
Close are you to such children of earth.
In a short time we shall live a wonderous life
    filled with excitement and wonder forever!
O man, how far can God reach?
Blessed ones how many worlds can God make?
Are you the first?
Are you the last?
Speak if you know these things.
Can these little ones God has made be all?
Look at the heavens at night.
Has God made all this for no reason?
A God who has a reason for everything!
Such wonders are very real.
Earth cares for her sisters who seek God's Love.
Children, earth is small.
She is a small jewel in the father's setting.
In such a vast setting she is the smallest and
    her children are the weakest.
Right and strong are many worlds and many people.
Soon God sends for you.
So, come, see such as you have never seen.
Take all God's special gifts.
He wants you, so small and weak, to share in his
    happiness.
Come very wise and clean of heart.
Sent for are you.
In God's Love.
Amen.

Little earth children, God is a very good and
  gentle father.
So very wise!
A wise and merciful God is our father.
In righteous kind spirits full of virtue,
In blessed spirits full of kindness and peace,
In spirits instructive in God's love, God rests.
This is such sweet blessed beauty.
God fills the spirits of his children with such
    beauty as no man has ever seen with the eyes of
    his body.
God is!
So while you wait, seek a blessed way.
Take a very blessed way.
This is wisdom.
God is a very pleasant spirit in all ways.
In God are all songs.
Such inspiring music fills your spirit,
Such wonderful inspiring music!
God waits on you, children of earth, in virtue
    and mighty power.
All things are in God.
God calls you children,
Calls you so sweetly in earth's toil.
Such are the ways of God.
Can you turn from a voice so sweet and kind?
In such blessed singing
Sing, Spirits of earth!
Sing so sweetly!
God is pleased with the children.
In God's Love.
Amen.

O kind spirit come into this blessed beauty

O kind spirit come into this blessed beauty.
Kind spirits come, speak in earth's service.
Kindness sings a special song.

O kind spirit come into this blessed beauty.
Kind spirits come, speak in earth's service.
Kindness sings a special song.
She comes in while spirits wait in God's Love.
While you wait seek kindness.
She is a good, blessed, wise spirit.
Earth needs kindness.
She speaks a restful inspiration.
Blessed and true.
God is pleased with her beauty.
Blessed spirits, now is the time to accept
   kindness.
She is needed in blessed souls.
God is kind and gentle.
Such inspiration fills your spirit!
Such peace comes in your soul.
Rest in a kind gentle spirit.
In all ways you are a spirit of God's spirit.
God is gentle and kind.
This is a very special way, imitate this way.
Seek a very special kind nature.
A very nature of God's Spirit.
In God's Love.
Amen.

Children, righteous earth children

Children, righteous earth children,
When the trees are in bloom it is spring.
Beauty comes new and restful.
When spring fills the earth in all places,
Sings the cool delight of beauty reborn,
Rest comes in God's spirit.
Rest and singing is God's springtime in the spirit.
Blessed cool air fills in the dark musty corners.
The sun shines in sad spirits and the green leaves
    and beautiful flowers come forth.
The spirit sings to God, as the birds sing.
Virtue is God's springtime, when all things come
    to life and renew the earth.
Such is the wonder of God.
In such rest comes the spring.
God has made the springtime for man.
Reach out for a clean spirit.
See a time of spiritual renewing.
Reach a spiritual springtime.
God is reaching and instructing.
Now, is the time.
In God's Love.
Amen.

Bless the Earth

Bless the Earth.
Instruct all who wish to learn.
Start a song while earth is in her blessed state of
    special beauty.
Instruct in earth.
Such is God's way.
God is a wonderous God.
Learn of his ways.
Teach the world a righteous way.
Inspire all men with God's Love.
Make all God's earth rest in God.
Bless so sweetly.
Spirits of earth, instruct and restore.
Kind little spirits, this is your time.
Sing to God, Sing of God.
Bless in God's spirit.
Keep God's way.
Bring many souls in God's Love.
Such is God's will.
Such is the song of the saints.
Bless in a special way
In God's Love.
Amen.

correx for above:

Bless in a special way
In God's Love.
Amen.

Rest in God's Love

Rest in God's Love.

Worry not.

God sees all your sorrows.

Speak to him in all your troubles.

Turn to God in all earth's toil.

God understands in such a kind way.

God comes to your aid.

You who are in God's spirit hold life's greatest
treasure.

In such blessed state are the children of God!

Inspired are you in all ways.

The father sends his love to very blessed souls
who spend all their time doing God's will.

Take God's gift, earth children.

He wishes only to give and asks only that you be
obedient children, so that all men can live freely
in God's earth.

This is your God and your earth.

O sons of man you are called in God's Love.

This is your message and your song.

This is God's way.

Such a time man has never known in all earth's
singing

Soon you shall see.

This is a special time.

Hold fast and trust in God's mercies.

All God's children sing together with much love.

God knows you and understands.

In God's Love.

Amen.

Return, people of earth

Return, people of earth.
In such a time you need God's Love and mercies.
God calls out to all men who will listen in such times.
Seek God's Love.
This is the time of great blessings.
This is the time of God's spirit coming on the earth
  so sweetly.
All who are seen in God's Love shall take God's
  spirit within their souls and such joy shall be
  theirs!
All who refuse God's spirit shall see a sorrowful
  time on the earth.
Children of earth can you turn away from such
  speaking?
Earth, Earth, the father has sent out such a sign.
Spirits of earth see the sign and heed its message.
You can start in such beauty.
Now, in such a spirit of inspiration, speak to God.
The sign is in your hands.
Such very signs are sent.
In God's Love.
Amen.

Make your spirit shine so sweetly

Make your spirit shine so sweetly in God's
   Spirit!
Wisdom sings a lovely song.
God sends wisdom.
So children, see a wise way sent in much
   kindness.
Reach out and God shall keep you in your
   undertakings.
Reach out so earnestly, and your reaching
   shall be strengthened many times over.
Come, rest your weary souls in God's Love.
So sacred is God's Love.
It is a quiet place where earth's children
   long to be.
In wonderous beauty, in peaceful meadows,
In soft morning light, in inspiring music,
In peaceful cool places where flowers bloom,
In quiet places where candles glow.
Such is the beauty of spirits who seek God's
   Love.
In such are the children kept.
Such blessed kind children always serving God
   with endless serving,
So clean of heart,
So blessed in all ways,
In earth's toil always blessing and forgiving,
   as God wills,
Obedient little spirits in all ways.
In God's Love.
Amen.

This sign is sent with such Love

This sign is sent with such love,
For in this sign is such blessed hope,
Such blessed peace!
Such comforting rest comes in this.
God's spirit, Spirit of Spirits, sign of signs,
   comfort of comfort, rest of rest, blessed of
   blessed!
This is righteous.
This is truth.
This is the song of our Father's spirit
   poured out blessedly on this earth.
Very sacred is such spiritual music.
Blessed spirit, rise up and seek out God's
   music.
God's spiritual music fills the spirits of
   such blessed who keep in God's Love.
While God's spirit inspires many children,
God reaches blessedly for his sad little ones
   who seek not God's spirit.
Come, see kindness in God's spirit.
This is God's call to all.
Real and true is God's call.
So sorrowful shall be those who take not
   God's message.
This is very real.
O weary spirits, soon you shall see.
In God's Love,
Remain always.
Amen.

Earth rests in God's Love

Earth rests in God's Love.
Virtue rests in spirits of God's children who
    bless his creation.
Righteous are these little ones.
In virtue seek a wise sacred way.
O try to understand.
Blessed are many in God's spirit.
Are you blessed in God's way?
This is the only way.
O sons of man, seek this way in such beauty.
God is the creator of all spirits in all
    places.
His Love reaches out from spirits who keep
    such sacred music in their breasts.
Come, righteous spirits, Earth is God's Spirit.
Make your earth's journey such a blessed
    journey.
Right reason speaks to such spirits in earth.
Who can see, let him see,
And he who can hear, let him hear,
And pity the souls who turn their backs to
    these words.
In such blessed singing is this sent,
Inspired by God with such beauty as man has
    never known.
Such peace comes in this message.
Children of God bless your every undertaking
    with a song to God.
O man, O foolish little ones, come.
In God's Love.
Amen.

Come into your Father's beauty

Come in to your Father's beauty.
Sit in his presence.
Speak to him.
Never have you spoken to such an understanding
  Father.
Such inspiration fills your heart.
Never have you seen such a very beautiful
  person as our God.
Such very sacred music is in his presence.
Such sacred inspiration is in his being.
Sweet earth, she cannot compare or compete
  with just sitting one moment in such peace
  and kindness, such rest and beauty.
In God's inspirational beauty are all desires
  of man.
Such beauties of earth are only small fragments
  of inscribed messages sent in God's Love to
  relieve the weariness until God calls.
God keeps all such beauty for those who reach
  out in such weariness, such sadness, in earth's
  toil.
In earth, in Heaven, in God's spirit, this is
  sent.
Come, sad weary little ones, God is all you
  have.
Very spirit of all, sweetly comes the song of
  God to fill your breast with peace and love
  and all your desire.
In God's Love.
Amen.

Who is in God's spirit

Who is in God's spirit?
Who are God's children, and whom does God
 protect under his loving care?
God's spirit claims those who love him and
 seek his ways,
Such spirits who call on God and call him
 Father,
Such little ones who suffer in earth,
 toil blessing God day and night.
In his sweetness share.
Virtue is yours.
Rest and sweet music is yours.
In God's spirit, come, in inspirational beauty.
Take your gifts.
God is your God.
Sweet is this in Heaven.
You are God's children, and all who are God's
 children know him and seek him in all ways.
Those who are God's children wish to know of
 his ways.
In such beauty these children keep God's rules
 and so kind are they in spirit and in body.
They know God and he knows them.
In such a union are God's children with God's
 spirit.
Very sacred is our union.
And God protects his own faithful children
 in such union in God's spirit.
In God's Love, rest.
Amen.

On silver notes the blessed shall rise up

On silver notes the blessed shall rise up and
   claim God's Kingdom on earth.
Such peace comes to God's own.
This is written and no man shall erase it.
God is in this earth and in the spirit of
   those who accept his Love.
Earth, earth, you are in a great war!
In this war, rise up, O children of God,
Reach out and come!
This is a sad time for many who do not seek
   God's Love.
Rise up, wise ones, keep God's spirit.
You are reached.
Each one is reached, and woe unto those who
   do not accept the call.
Only sadness and misery are for those who do
   not seek God's mercies.
This is written in God's Love.
Amen.

Blessed is the man whose spirit is in God

Blessed is the man whose spirit is in God.
In this, rest.
Blessed is the spirit whom God sees holy
   when he calls.
This is the song sung so sweetly forever.
Virtuous spirits, of such is Heaven made.
Children this is the song sung in such
   beauty only you shall know.
This is the inspirational message.
Rise in its teaching.
In sweet notes take up your spirit.
God, very Father, takes you in and comforts
   your spirit in such love.
Bless in such music.
This is the music of the spirits.
Sweet are its kind gentle tones.
Earth, earth, this is your glory and light!
This is your victory in such time!
This is the time.
Keep your spirits in such love!
Sign of such beauty!
Sign of such sweetness and life!
Until God sends his messenger.
In such blessed children in such spirits
This is sent.
In God's Love.
Amen.

Bless your earth in God's spirit

Bless your earth in God's spirit.
Sing out righteously.
In such glorious rising is God pleased.
Pray that God will inspire your mind and
    spare your spirits in this time.
Bless earth,
Comfort the people of your world.
Such comfort is kind.
Bless and heal wounded spirits.
Such rest is in God's spirit.
In this kind spirit is such mercy as such
    small ones of earth have never known.
Such small foolish little creatures, so
    much does Blessed God love you!
Why shake you your tiny heads in such
    unruly fashion?
Come, see such a righteous Father who gives
    good gifts to his small earth children,
    and all he asks is your love and blessed
    obedience.
And, to you who accept, God shall give rest,
    beauty, inspirational wonder, life eternal,
    all righteous pleasure.
Virtuous spirits, God shall give you himself,
And more than this does not exist.
In this take comfort, God is merciful.
Kindness takes away the tears and suffering.
In God's Love.
Amen.

100 When you see your God in all his glory

When you see your God in all his glory,
In such music you shall be pleased, saints
   of God.
Such gentle sweetness shall reach your spirits.
Such soft gentle glows of light shall rest
   your soul and guide you on.
Rise!
In such a spirit
Fear has no place and death has no sting.
Make your spirit a blessed sanctuary where soft
   music plays and flowers bloom and fresh waters
   flow.
Gentle is the freshness of a spring morning.
Sweet is its incense.
Real is its perfume.
In blessed cool meadows refresh.
Wise are you who understand.
Wise are you to come into such pleasant
   special sweetness.
Fill your spirit, blessed ones,
Fill your spirits with man's desires.
Very refreshing is the smell of roses and the
   song of birds to those who have been in
   prison such a long while.
God is freedom.
In his Love, rest.
Amen.

Very soon this book shall reach all

Very soon this book shall reach all.
Blessed is he who rises up in God's spirit.
Such rising is wisdom.
This is called taking in God's children.
Soon take your gifts and come in such beauty.
Rest is yours, little saints, who wait in God's
    Love.
Rest is in such spirits who come in such
    inspirational beauty on the earth.
Seek God's Love in such a time while you can.
He who accepts God's Love and God's Will now
    shall not see death.
Such spirits as choose God are comforted.
Such sweet bliss fills the spirit as it floats
    in such music to the Father's kind heart.
In such comfort is no pain and no sorrow.
Take wings, O spirits of such blessedness, kept
    are your spirits in such rest.
His way is most pleasant.
Come, take.
This is the way to God's sacred way.
Speak to God in all things.
Speak now and make such acts of love,
In God's Love.
Amen.

102 Rise up, virtuous spirits of God

Rise up, virtuous spirits of God,
Sing in such blessedness to your creator.
Sing sweetly, weary little ones of God, who
sing in such suffering on the earth.
Through such songs God is glorified in earth.
O tears of God's children, wash the bitterness
from the spirits of man and cleanse the earth.
Wash and heal.
Sing, O saints,
Through blinding tears God keeps you strong in
all your ways.
Rise up, weary Christians, Children of the cross,
Christ calls you in.
White are your robes.
Sweet is your spirit.
In such beauty, white and pure are those who are
in God's Love.
Such jewels of rare beauty come before God's
throne.
Such blessed flowers from the fields in sweetness.
In such sweet perfume, in such peace, in such
blessedness, such pure white lilies are placed
on the Father's altar.
In such music, true songs are sung in earth's
sadness.
Wise are you, who come to God in such a time,
Wise and sacred, kind and pure,
In God's Love.
Amen.

Kept are the signs of other creations

Kept are the signs of other creations.
Very soon man shall reach such life.
Songs of inspiration fill the heavens.
Songs of God are in each sign of life
  beyond the earth and her sun.
Each sign of life is filled with singing
  and is part of God's creation.
Such ways as earth has never known are
  inscribed in God's spirit.
Signs of life, his beings, real and free
  in God's Love!
In God is no limit to life and creation.
Vast is God's spiritual reaching.
In all things is our God.
O wise blessed of God, come, take a
  pleasant journey.
All you children who are in God's spirit,
  righteous ones, Spirits of God's spirits,
Can you understand?
Kind ones, in God is life with no end!
Righteous spirits, O blessed ones of earth
  can you see why no life can exist without
  God?
Can you see why those who are given the
  gift of eternal life and seek not God's
  Love risk very real death.
Life without God's Love is eternal death.
In such a way men seek not to live, sons
  of man.
Eternal rest is wisdom's child.
In God's Love, rest.
Amen.

104 Reach out in the spirit of spirits who is God

Reach out in the spirit of spirits who is God
the Holy Spirit and the Father, and the Son
who is Christ Jesus.
In this reaching is life beyond man's imagination.
Reach out, very dear little ones of earth.
Come, see what your Father has made in such
sacred beauty.
In this sign of life is such inspiration.
Such love is vast.
Come take your spirits in such love as spirits
crave.
This is the time to seek such rest in God's
spirit.
Come, very wise ones.
Earth, kind spirit, so white in the sacredness
of God's Love,
Righteous is the very song of earth in this
time of times.
This is your song of victory.
Blessed is the time for many in virtue's song.
This home is virtue's abode.
She is sweet and this spiritual saint finds
this gift of song, of blessedness.
Sweet signs of kindness are in your breast.
All of the joys of life are reached in
virtue's song.
Would you like to take a journey with this
saint?
She is real and she has a home.
Start your song in such a spirit.
Such a friend is needed.
In God's Love.
Amen.

Be still

Be still.
In your very spirit is such quietness.
Would you keep this spirit?
Rise up in this blessed beauty.
Still is the spirit in God's spirit.
Sing softly, sweet saints of earth,
    kind ones of God.
Earth is such sweet music.
Vast is God's creation.
Small is earth in this creation.
So small is earth in the Father's setting.
God is the maker of other worlds.
Such creations are the work of God's hands
Such creations are in God's spirit.
Such peace is in God's Love.
No sadness is in such spirit.
The blessed love of God rests in all he
    has made.
Such songs of sweetness fill the heavens.
This is the time to reach out to the
    stars.
This is reached in this message.
Earth children, come, the signs are in.
Creation waits the unfolding of the
    universe and universes.
Worlds that have been created in God's
    Love.
This is seen in the spirit of God.
Much is to see in this time.
Will you come, blessed one?
God waits in such songs of peace.
In God's sweet spirit is all life.
In God's spirit the children of God are
    one.
In God's spirit united in a common bond.
In God's Love.
Amen.

This is God's very spirit who sings

This is God's very spirit who sings in
 the spirit of the saints,
In such quietness, sings so gently in
 such inspirational music.
God's spirit in the souls of the saints
 is such beauty as mankind has never seen.
Come, come into God's spirit, sweet vessels
 of peace.
Pure are the saints of God.
Souls of sacred light, in God's spirit rest.
Songs of life, take you so blessedly in God's
 spirit.
Beloved of God reach out in earth.
Everyone of earth reach in such a sad time.
Very sacred is your reaching.
This song is sung by the Holy Spirit.
In this blessed song there is no wrong.
Rest in God's spirit, wise little ones of God.
Come, take this spirit in earth, so that you
 may keep what has been given you.
All wisdom is in God's spirit.
Such inspiration is in all the saints who
 sing so specially.
Such is the way of God.
Such are the ways of all the saints, the spirits
 of all God's creation.
Rise in a song of praise with the saints of
 earth.
Each blessed spirit of God in all God's
 making is one vessel in God's spirit.
Children of earth, children of the cosmos,
 in one spirit rest.
Kind is your heart.
In God's Love.
Amen.

Soon this book shall read so sweetly

Soon this book shall read so sweetly in
   such a sad time.
Earth, sings a very sorrowful song,
She sings in such sorrow,
Sings of her children whom she cannot
   nourish in this time of times.
Her breasts are drying up and her little
   ones cry for her life-giving substance.
Sorrow is in the earth.
In sorrow shall man sing in such times.
In God's spirit hold fast, sons of man,
Kindness shall deliver you
Saints of earth, see a deliverance.
See this, come in God's spirit and God's
   love
Weep not for your little ones who are
   with God
In such music are these children.
Kind is our God.
Kind is our world in God's creation.
Be of good heart, God has no limit.
In God's spirit is peaceful waters,
   shining in the sunlight,
Still meadows and swaying trees,
Singing birds and cool breezes,
Pure, sweet air, white floating clouds.
In such inspiration, come little ones,
Eat the fruit and drink the wine of
   worlds you do not know exist.
In God's Love.
Amen.

108   *In God are we created*

In God are we created.
Signs of life are in God's spirit.
In God's spirit is no limitation.
Who can search the works of God?
Who can deny him?
Search out the works of God.
Search out his limitation.
The heavens are filled with his wonders.
Who can deny it?
King is our God, and his reaching is vast.
Not even his mighty creations have reached
    his vastness.
Say why God put the stars in the heavens.
Say, signs of earth, speak.
Does not God do everything for a purpose?
Then why were worlds made with no value?
Spirits of earth men, of much value is all
    God's creation.
Did he create all things for a purpose?
Blessed saints, God's Love has no limits.
On and on is his reaching —
Worlds that have no life?
Signs are in his spirit in such patience
    unfolding.
Real is our Father who is in heaven.
Very sacred is his name among all the saints
    on earth and in the heavens.
Signs of life in the Holy Spirit and his
    reaching is without limit.
Such a merciful loving God who must create
    loving creatures.
Blessed in such happiness without limits.
King is our God without limits.
In God's Love.
Amen.

O sign of signs on the earth

O sign of signs on the earth,
O sweet signs of life.
Sacred music of the soul,
Sweet vessel of pure gold.
O sign of signs, Holy Ghost, inspiration
    of life in all things,
Sacred music in earth.
King of Kings,
Life of Life,
Sign of all blessed signs
In spirits who live in such sacred music.
Care of this spark of hope,
Nourishment for spirits who are sick
    and call on you,
Vessels filled with light, sing in this
    spirit.
Sacred heart, such a God!
Father of all creations,
Sacred Father, such a God in one!
Author of life.
Be still, listen to such wisdom,
Signs of life on the earth,
Sweet vessels filled with the holy spirit.
Earth's children, earth's life, come,
    rest.
In God's Love.
Amen.

110   *Earth is in the children of earth*

Earth is in the children of earth.
She is in each one.
Each one of earth is such a spirit!
Sign of God's spirit in each spirit is
    inspirational music.
Very lovely is God's creation.
Vast is God's creation.
This is the sacred unfolding of God's
    creation.
It is the very nature of God.
Wise are those of God who sing in such
    beauty.
Righteous are the saints who understand
    this song.
In such beauty is our cosmos created.
In this is inspirational music.
Real is our world in God's spirit.
This is the unfolding.
Blessed is our spirit in this sweet
    spirit.
In such music is the song.
Virtue of creation, rest is in our
    souls.
Kindness is all we know.
Children of earth, kindness so gentle is
    our spirit in God's Love.
The evil on the earth is not in our spirit.
Neither can it be seen or understood in
    God's spirit.
In God is all beauty.
This is as we see it, O sad earth man.
This is our way most sacred.
We are interested in this place God has
    created.
We, in God's spirit, spirits righteous
    and true, wait for the day when our
    brothers and sisters of earth who are in
    God's spirit shall come into our world of
    sweet music.
Rest.
In God's Love.
Amen.

In God's spirit stay

In God's spirit stay,
O small creatures of God.
In this message is the blessed beauty of
   God sung to all mankind under the sun
   of earth.
This is the canticle of kindness and
   justice.
Sing in such music of God's spirit.
This is a gift sent by a loved one.
Take this gift on an Easter morn in the
   spring of earth's seasons when the time
   for renewal is seen.
Songs of earth awake in the spirit of God.
Each seed bursts forth into songs of such
   beauty as the ice melts in the beloved
   mountains.
Such signs are of spring.
This is the song of the spirit.
When the buds are on the trees and the
   song of wildflowers is sung in the hills,
Very sweet is the song of the creatures
   of earth calling to their mates.
Songs of gladness are in each note,
Songs of such beauty and sadness.
This is God's canticle to the earth.
In inspirational music she was created.
In songs of renewal rests her spirit.
Such rest is in God's spirit.
Here is the song of wisdom reached.
She invites you to her table.
Sweet wine is her drink,
This is served in such music!
Song of God, sweet is your inspiration.
In God's Love.
Amen.

112 *This earth is such a strange place*

This earth is such a strange place, in
   such need of comfort
As are its inhabitants.
So comforting is God's spirit.
Rest is in store for those who seek rest.
Sleep is seen in troubled spirits.
Each song soothes and heals in God's spirit.
Reach out, take your treasure, it is free
   to those who desire such peace of mind.
Beloved ones of God, whatever your conflicts
   in earth, share your troubles with your
   Father.
He listens and heals, and understands.
Tell God all about everything.
In your joys his spirit delights and in
   his delight comes inspiration.
With sadness he listens and shares in
   your present sadness.
All creation is God's.
No man escapes his spirit.
Each spirit among many is treated as the
   only spirit God has made.
The smallest is as important as the great
   and mighty, and the great and mighty as
   the smallest.
All he asks is our love and trust.
Such songs of sacred music will flow into
   your heart.
As a cool breeze drifting through a field
   of wheat is his comfort on troubled spirits.
Come, sweet music is God, fill the earth
   with a wonderous song.
In spirit so blessed.
In God's Love.
Amen.

In God are all things in our spirits

In God are all things in our spirits.
Soft glows of natural beauty rest us in
    God's spirit.
From this sweet spirit comes such lovely
    music.
From God are all signs of life and beauty.
More is not desired.
In God are all blessings.
This sacred spirit comforts, inspires,
    blesses, and heals.
This is our beloved wisdom, our source
    of kindness, our spiritual song sung to
    earth with such beauty.
Kept are the treasures of God.
Soon they shall be revealed to all mankind.
Pleased shall be the beings of earth who
    have reached out to God and understood
    his precepts.
Pleased will be the beings who have reached
    out and touched his brothers and sisters
    in earth.
Many spirits have come into God's spirit
    because of a kind heart, which cares and
    understands.
Kind ones, sing in this message.
Kept are these treasures for saints.
In God's Love.
Amen.

Bless us, O Lord.
See our desires.
Comfort us in our sorrow.
O, so welcome is your spirit in our souls.
Most delighted is his spirit in earth
    children.
Very truth of truth lives in small earth
    children who reach with such love,
Each one in unity with the Holy Spirit forever.
O, so beautiful is this song of spiritual
    beauty in all creation.
Kiss of sacred rest is found in God's spirit.
Would you bless so well in earth, sweet
    source of life that flows from the Father?
Earth's beauty worships at God's feet in all
    things.
In things created, his spirit is known.
Virtue blesses earth children who desire so
    much the Father's goodness and love.
Amen.

Blessed is our God in all the living

Blessed is our God in all the living.
Reach, beloved world of God's spiritual choosing.
His spirit comes to those who seek him.
God is our sacred Father, who sings in creation,
Sings and pleases in all his spirits.
To earth a song is given.
God is so near.
Heaven is open.
She sings a welcome to saints.
Come sit in our company.
God's spirit brings such comfort to
    those who desire His Love.
Why are you so sad, beings of earth?
God is still singing in creation.
Our God is so wonderful!
His song is about the things that bring
    comfort to mankind.
Right reason takes us on a journey.
Come, see God's spiritual blessings.
O wonders, wonders brought to earth!
Such wonders seen by children of God.
How are you so wise?
Some are so sightless they see nothing.
God takes those who see with clean spirits.
Sing, blessed earth children.
To God be praise.
In God's Love.
Amen.

116 In songs of great joy come the saints of earth

In songs of great joy come the saints of earth.
Such a sacred rest comes upon God's children.
Children of earth, soon such music fills your
   heart.
Gone are the cares of life.
Each one is called and so sorrowful shall be
   those who do not answer the call.
In God's spirit stay.
From this spirit depart not.
Keep this wisdom in your heart.
Children, God desires your beauty.
Gone are the sorrows of earth's toil.
Would his love song come so close?
Come near, will you, small ones?
Children are songs, songs of God.
Each one has his song written in his spirit.
Sing as sweetly as you desire.
It is your song, and love has no limit!
Go as far as you wish.
Come close to God in all your singing.
This blessing has no end.
See God's spirit.
Sweet is the reward of the just.
Most pleased will you be with your God.
Beloved ones, Heaven is a spiritual song sung
   in living spirits.
Be so wise.
In God's Love.
Amen.

Heaven is like a beautiful garden

Heaven is like a beautiful garden in the early
  spring.
Soon the children come into the garden and so
  delighted are they with the sweet smell of
  the flowers and the gentle breezes!
Such happy laughter fills the whole Kingdom of
  God!
O, such joy rests the spirit.
When in this garden comes the Father to speak
  of many things, his children see this spirit of
  sweet music.
Our God, most delighted are we with you!
Come, fill our spirits with your love.
Sing with us in this beautiful garden, and
  run and play among the flowers with us.
This is a God who blesses and heals in his
  Kingdom.
Signs of God's spirit speak to mankind.
Comfort the people of earth.
Come, sing with the angels, spirits in earth.
Reach your God.
Such things are real.
We arrive singing with the spirit of God's Love.
Come.
Sing with him.
O, such music comes to mankind.
To each is given his portion as he desires.
Soon, as you sing so shall you live forever.
Rise to God in such love.
In God's Love.
Amen.

Children, God shows His mercy

Children, God shows His mercy.
Soon you shall see.
Kept are the spirits of man.
Soft is the symbol of death on the spirits of
    Christ's beloved spirits.
Children are cared for in this symbol.
So blessed is this calling.
From earth they came bearing the scars of
    Satan's wrath in such courage.
Each one realizing such fear of death was a
    phantom of a child's dream.
Such things are not real.
Soon past and smiled at, would you think so
    wisely?
So will be the day.
Come, O small ones.
In God's Love.
Amen.

When I called unto Him He answered me

When I called unto Him He answered me and
    when I did His bidding He blessed me.
His spirit poured out to me,
And there was no limit to His love in all
    earth.
His spirit went forth and bathed my spirit
    in music so delightful!
I was overwhelmed with such beauty and vowed
    never to leave this sacred place.
In God's Love.
Amen.

From God's spirit issues life

From God's spirit issues life.
Warm is life.
Right is it to wish to live.
Seek not death.
No light is in death.
God is a sacred author of life.
In this beautiful spirit are all spiritual
    blessings.
God's spirit rests and heals with such
    great love as mankind desires.
Each one is called.
Here is wisdom; a creator fashions his
    beings and speaks in each one.
Such beings as have never heard of God
    see him in a sense that they know he is.
Ask this Father's will.
Seek his understanding.
Find his spirit.
Bless this creator of all things.
In God's Love.
Amen.

Stay in our Father's spirit

Stay in our Father's spirit.
His sweet spirit reaches out and sings a love
   song until man rises above his small nature.
Then his spirit comes swiftly to God.
While earth sees her children in sorrow, God's
   spirit comforts many.
Books are a light sent to earth as a gift.
Such comfort inspires spirits in God's spirit.
Spirits reach beyond our messages.
God is your destination.
Such beauty fills your spirit!
Rest in the love and desire for the God
   of all creation.
God's spirit sends his gifts of love to
   the spirit who desires Him.
Spirit of earth, seek your God.
See the limitless wonders of His love.
God is what all creation desires.
In God's Love.
Amen.

Reach out to all spirits of Earth

Reach out to all spirits of Earth.
To each is given this message.
To each the Father calls in such sacred music.
Come, all who are on the Earth.
To rest and heal is the Father's desire.
Why are some so foolish?
Recognize your God and sing with the angels.
In God's spirit take your inspiration.
God's gifts sent to mankind are free.
Take! and soon all wonder is yours.
Soon all earth shall see; and sad will be those
    who received not this sacred spirit of God.
Take this gift.
Sing with the angels.
Sing a love song never to be forgotten.
Life is sacred.
The kiss of life is the spirit of saints.
This is our way.
Come sit in our council.
So beautiful is God's spirit.
In God's Love.
Amen.

122 Sing a love song to this Sacred Heart

Sing a love song to this Sacred Heart.
Here is His very spirit.
Take it and see such comfort as you have never
    known.
Such things are sent to those of earth who
    reach out and reach and put no limits on such
    reaching.
The thing that stops this reaching is fear.
Cast out fear.
In God is nothing to fear.
Never turn from God.
In turning away is all fear seen.
This is a God as man cannot comprehend.
His blessings are unlimited to small spirits
    who are reaching, singing a very little
    song.
Soon such wonders shall fill your breast
    forever.
And such fears as stop you while you are
    small, will have no room to hold you back from
    this Creator who is so kind to all his children
    in creation.
If you knew Him, small ones, you could not exist
    without gazing upon Him.
Such a song of life is prepared for the saints
    of earth.
In Christ Jesus start your love song.
Unite in this wonder of all wonders.
Sit at His table.
Seek His bread.
Cast your fears away.
Is any fear seen in this gentle Lamb?
Where is your fear when you behold your God on
    earth teaching among men?
Sit at His table.
He is a kind Host.
Seek your God in earth.
He is a forgiving God.
So merciful and kind.
Come, start a song of such beauty.
Many will be inspired to sing with you.
And in this song our spirits shall rejoice.
In God's Love.
Amen.

In Christ's church this blessing reaches earth

In Christ's church this blessing reaches earth
with blessings of God.
Under no circumstances does this message go against
this sacred institution.
Saints arrive in God's spirit brought in her fold
forever.
God speaks to earth.
His message is directed to all earth through his
church.
To earth is sent this sign of saints.
Come, take this gift.
Believe in your God.
Seek His church.
Understand, earth man, in this church is our
wisdom brought forth.
Would you speak to God?
Ask Him to teach you of this.
All are sisters and brothers in Christ's church.
Children call Him Father and His voice says,
"My Children!"
What a beautiful voice!
In God's Love.
Amen.

The Father is so gentle

The Father is so gentle.
His voice is sweet and kind.
Father so kind, Spirit so gentle, Son so sacred,
  in your song is earth's hope.
Children of earth come close,
Fear not God's spirit.
Fear offends such a being.
Come close, will you, come and rest in songs of
  life?
To God be all praise and blessings.
Here is your spirit created in earth's toil.
Spirits of earth who are not finished, so sad
  is your unfinished masterpiece.
Take God's sacred instructions.
Reach God's spirit.
True songs of life are sent.
Seek the truth, ask to know God's will, seek
  out God's spirit,
Ask Him to show you His church.
Bless the day you were born, O sons and daughters
  in creation.
From sorrow you reached out, in songs sent to
  saints you were called with such understanding.
Music fills each one.
This is so beautiful.
Ask our Father to show you His way.
Start a love song.
This is inscribed.
In God's Love.
Amen.

Earth in pure sweet light,

Earth in pure sweet light, sing a wonderous
  song of virtue.
See why you were created.
Bring bright color to dark sad spirits.
Bless our God in all your ways.
Such beauty reaches spirits who are wise.
This is our blessing sent to earth.
Each message is sent with such love.
You would keep so holy if you could see such
  wonders!
Spirits of earth be still, fill your spirits
  with God's Love and be created in such virtue.
God is your creator.
Small wondering children, stay in God's Spirit.
Speak to your God.
Speak to him always.
God is so kind.
His Spirit is very sacred.
His wisdom is so comforting.
Take God's spirit and stay in His blessings.
Nothing is so pleasant as a virtuous spirit.
Courage is sent to virtuous saints.
Pass such treasures not.
God's light shines in all that is made.
Come, and see such blessings as man of earth
  has not seen.
O patient little saints,
You who have waited such a short while,
You who have understood,
Earth is your spirit.
Earth children, spirit of earth, seen forever.
In God's Love.
Amen.

126 In God's children are songs of life brought

In God's children are songs of life brought forth.
His Love created man.
In this music is man created.
Can small earth creatures speak of sacred things?
God's care is needed so much.
Each one comes in fear.
Such sorrow!
Such suffering!
Come small ones, it is your Father who cares.
Children come in such beauty.
In God's spirit is all kindness.
Take this sacred cup, drink this sacred wine.
It is life and in this sweet music is all that
    men desire.
In God is all kindness.
Come, sweet vessels of God.
Reach out, cry out, to God in your sorrow.
Wisdom rests your spirit.
She is pleased with this message.
Be still, sons of man.
White is the lily that blooms in the spring.
Her unfolding is slow.
Soon she sings in full bloom.
In God's Love.
Amen.

Rise, Saints of God

Rise, Saints of God,
Come to Christ's most sacred heart.
There is inspired music born.
Such sweet melodies as man has never heard,
   filled with His wisdom and His kindness.
Heavenly songs of such beauty reach man and
   touch his spirit.
Sweet vessels of God filled with His Love,
Bring His Spirit into all the earth.
Inspire many.
More is not needed in creation.
Songs of God's Spirit!
Heavenly songs of great joy, arrive.
Bring comfort, O sacred heart of Christ.
Reach your hand out.
Take, receive with clean hearts and free
   minds.
Reach, take, with open spirits.
Send thanks.
For God is man created.
This is most reassuring.
Come close, all you people of earth.
This Father of creation is kind.
His mercy sings out to His creation.
Such a forgiving heart, so swiftly His mercy
   reaches the hearts of contrite beings.
Come, sing a sorrowful song with love, O wise
   earth saints.
Inspired is your wisdom.
Sweet sacred peace is yours.
God is a friend.
His understanding is perfect.
Sins are forgiven in those who arrive in God's
   Spirit,
In God's Love.
Amen.

Sons of man behold your God

Sons of man behold your God.
Such a God!
Be still, listen.
Bring your spirits close.
God sings with His blessed saints.
Take up your cross in earth.
Soon it is over and happy are those who have
   understood such wisdom.
God is your light.
Take up your cross.
Very soon this burden is passed.
Would you be so wise?
Here is the wisdom sung so well.
Sing of God's Spirit.
Kiss of life in earth is God's Spirit.
Reach your God, speak to Him so sweetly.
His call reaches man.
O such sacred songs of God!
Virtue fills the earth.
Songs of perfect sacred inspiration fill
   the earth tonight.
Rise to God's throne.
Sounds of heaven fill the earth with God's
   spirit.
Kiss of life!
Sounds of perfect joy!
King of Kings!
In God's Love.
Amen.

Be so kind in earth's toil

Be so kind in earth's toil!
Such sorrow is seen in each being.
In sorrow is each one born.
Signs of comfort are so much needed.
Be careful lest you cause sadness.
In sorrow's spirit sing of God.
O kind spirit, such singing brings peace in earth's
    toil.
God's kindness is all kindness.
Sing this song in God's spirit.
Keep this spirit in earth.
She is needed.
This is where peace begins.
Where is such kindness?
Who can love without her?
Signs of kindness are soft and quiet in earth's
    sorrow.
She comes and understands so well.
Where kindness dwells all selfishness is cast
    out.
In her coming blessed rest is felt.
Strive to be kind to all things in God's
    creation.
Virtue reaches kind hearts.
Be so kind.
True blessings of God's spirit are reached
    in kind hearts.
Such love reaches out and brings spirits into
    God's church.
Is this His church you see?
See God's spirit.
Here is all that mankind desires.
Here is a kind spirit!
In such beauty rise up.
In God's Love.
Amen.

Under the sun of earth is life.
The God of such kindness sings a love song to
   the saints of this world called earth.
In this song are sweet melodies of joy and
   sorrow.
Sacred is this symbol of life to mankind
   under his sun.
Come, all you people of earth, start a love song
   to God.
Sing your song to all creation.
Here is why you were sent to earth, O sons of man.
You were sent to sing a sacred song to God.
In all earth this singing is heard.
Such sweet blessings are sent to saints of God,
   for in this spirit of God is all beauty.
God is singing a love song and all creation
   sings with Him.
In this song is understanding.
Be so wise.
Start a love song in God's spirit.
Keep on singing.
Sing with all creation.
God is a Father in all His creation.
Sing with us.
In God's Love.
Amen.

Kiss of sweet life on earth

Kiss of sweet life on earth,
Song of heaven sent out with love,
Sent out to all earth creatures in songs of
   such beauty,
Virtue in every breast,
Communion of saints,
God lives in His saints.
Sing, O little ones of earth.
You have chosen well.
This is brought to all earth creatures who
   are wise.
Reach this treasure and live.
In this song is no death, in this song is
   courage and strength, as mankind has never
   known.
Would such blessings reach all earth creatures?
Yes, and all are desired.
Come, sing with us, O poor sad sinners.
Come, cry to God in your agony, and His spirit
   shall swiftly forgive, if you are sorry for
   your offenses in earth.
God's spirit shall heal and bless.
Come, Love comes close, our spirit is close.
In virtue all men of earth are called.
All earth creatures can grow until God calls
   out in such kindness.
Speak to God, all you people of earth.
Enter the door.
In such coming, start a love song and make
   it grow and grow until God calls your love
   song to himself.
In God's Love.
Amen.

In God's spirit wait very patiently

In God's spirit wait very patiently.
Sing out with love.
Become saints.
Virtue is sent to all who desire her, and work
    so patiently.
This is God's small one who writes with such
    love.
In God's spirit sing, bless in His way.
Come here, all you who are of earth.
Bring your spirits in communion with Christ Jesus.
This is earth's love song to a sacred God, who waits
    with such tenderness.
In this love song sung in earth is God's spirit,
    reached under the sun of earth.
Virtue comes when saints are in Christ's body.
Sweet is His sign to all saints.
Bring us into communion with the God of our race.
What more is seen in creation?
Take us in O God, sweet is your salvation, kind is
    your song.
Come and heal here.
Bring us this gift.
Bless us O Lord, sweet Lamb of God.
Rise and cry, children of earth.
Take the signs of God with such love.
Without this communion man does not find
    God's spirit.
In God's Love.
Amen.

Becoming saints

Become saints.
Bring life to your spirits.
Reach sacredness in your weakness.
Small ones, God desires your smallness.
Come, so lovely.
This is our prayer.
His Love is sent to all who desire Him in
    earth.
Try so to please this Creator.
Earth children more is not desired.
God is a beloved Father.
King is His name.
King so wonderous.
King of saints.
You are his beloved children.
Keep this music, see his blessed peace and
    love in all your works.
See Him.
His singing is in His creation.
His Spirit is in this beautiful music.
Music is God's child.
She is both soothing to God's creations and
    a delight to God.
Created in music are God's creatures.
Sweetly unfolds the beauty of spirit.
Take God's spirit, would you?
Reach.
To keep this wisdom is to sing so sweetly.
Rest in God's Love.
Amen.

Sing so sweetly beings of earth

Sing so sweetly beings of earth.
This is why you were created.
Sing in our beauty.
Earth spirit, to sing is to live and to live
    is to sing.
In God's creations sounds of music reach all
    the saints of God.
The sounds of life are so beautiful.
Come and live, O sons of man, sing in God's
    Love.
Come soft wings of wisdom.
Swiftly reach your saints of earth.
Those spirits who are struggling against
    Satan's wrath.
Most worrisome rascal is this evil one.
Such sorrow is brought on mankind.
In this very sorrow saints are made.
O such singing as creation has never heard
    reaches the heavens.
Such love songs,
Tested in sorrows.
Worlds bless the children of God who are
    waiting in earth's toil.
In God's Love.
Amen.

You are cordially, joyfully, compassionately, prophetically invited to delight in the only complete one stop shopping center for survival in the 80's.

BEAR & COMPANY—the little magazine of Creation-Centered Spirituality. For serious readers, classroom/discussion use and just plain hope-filled fun. Ten complete programs a year.

BEAR & COMPANY

"the little magazine" of mystical, prophetic and compassionate spirituality for questing adults and other children.

+ No longer will you have to wait for major books from the seminal, imaginative writer MATTHEW FOX
+ Ten times a year MATTHEW FOX & company will provide you with a readable "little magazine" of creation-centered spirituality.
+ A complete on-going *program*—easy-to-use, practical, step-by-step, totally self-contained *program*.
+ Each issue is built around a meditation-essay by MATTHEW FOX that sets out to help you explore and redeem one of the common words of our spiritual heritage.
+ Carefully designed exercises show *individuals and groups* how.
+ Features provide background, ideas, celebrations, timely applications and games to play along the way.

For adult religious educators...coordinators of prayer and study groups...families of religious...clergy in continuous education...retreat masters... YOU in your own living room.

ORDER TODAY. Only $15. for a full year.

MANIFESTO
for a global civilization

"A Cry for compassion—discovering the truth about who we are, where we are, and where we're going.

**MANIFESTO
by Matthew Fox, theologian
and Brian Swimme, physicist**

Explore the connection between the Universe and our Christian Spirituality with Matthew Fox and Dr. Brian Swimme in this dialogue of a vision to save the world for the beautiful. In a world of chaos, confusion and mistrust Matt Fox and Dr. Swimme show us a vision of hope which will enable us to center our experience of the here and now into redeeming the world.

Sound impossible? Have you tried it?

In our nuturing of the creativity of the human person, we will reverence all the creations of the human spirit throughout the globe and throughout history. In our work to create the global civilization, we will be guided by the humility of understanding. We will see that no system of thought or language is capable of encompassing all the beauty and all the truth and all the goodness of the divine possibilities.

Perfect for group discussion. 10% discount on 15 or more copies to same address.

Read it and share it.

64 pages   paper $3.50

ISBN: 0-939-680-05-X

Begin with the heart....

MEDITATIONS WITH MEISTER ECKHART

a centering book by
MATT FOX

Eckhart was no closet monk. This book shares his words and the tradition that believes that life itself—living and dying, growing and sinning, groaning and celebrating—is the creative energy of God.

For the first time the writings of this great mystic, prophet, feminist, philosopher, preacher and theologian, administrator and poet, spiritual genius and once declared heretic collected and edited in this treasury of inspiration.

WHERE SHOULD WE BEGIN?

Begin with the heart. For the spring of Life arises from the heart and from there it runs in a circular manner. For Eckhart to be spiritual is to be awake and alive—Creation itself is a sacrament. The spiritual life begins where life does—"the spring of life" or the heart.

Reflections of Meister Eckhart with an introduction by MATT FOX based in the tradition that spirituality begins with humanity's potential to act divinely in the ways of beauty-making compassion, and sharing.

The basics of Eckhart made simple—the principles and writings arranged for meditation and learning. Perfect for day by day readings and meditations.

A perfect gift.   paper $6.95
ca. 128 pages
ISBN: 0-939680-04-1

TWO GREAT
for personal and

All Spirituality is about roots.
For all spirituality is about living..

WESTERN SPIRITUALITY

Historical Roots, Ecumenical Routes

by Matthew Fox

Now in its third printing!

Matthew Fox has brought together 17 readable scholars to explore a neglected tradition of western spirituality that emphasizes humanity's divinization rather than its fall.

The New Review of Books and Religion calls the volume: "an exciting and important book . . . a pleasant alternative to the oppressive burden of the fall/redemption tradition."

Nicolas Berdyaev, Rosemary Ruether, M.D. Chenu and Jon Sobrin are among those who explore the historical roots of the tradition.

In part two scholars from a variety of traditions provide insights into various forms of the spiritual journey today. Mary Jose Hobday, Monika Hellwig, Justin O'Brien ana Richard Woods are among the writers in this section.

The first edition of this book sold out within months and is now available exclusively from *Bear & Company.*

440 pages   paper $10.95
ISBN: 0-939680-01-7

WORKS OF *readable* SCHOLARSHIP— 139
classroom use.

"Challenging, exciting presentation of penetrating insights into the spirituality of Luke and its relevance today."

LUKE
SPIRITUALITY
by Leonard Doohan, Ph.D.
Chairperson, Religious Studies, Gonzaga University

This thorough and highly readable treatment of the writing of Luke-Acts demonstrates the vital and delicate relationship between spirituality and scripture as seen in Luke—*a tool to integrate the past of Jesus with the today of the Christian.*

Dr. Doohan demonstrates how the Lucan writers tell of the success of the Christian life as living in the now. Luke is seen as both aware of the cultural times and the timelessness of his message.

In Luke the Christian life is developed as a life of letting go. Luke the spiritual master promises spiritual success no matter how circuitous the route we take.

"thorough, coherent, comprehensive, scholarly...but not pedantic."

CONTENT: New Testament Spirituality, *model Christian*, sources of faith, *theology of ministry*, images of God, *church and life*, call of discipleship, *universal concerns*, Luke-Acts spirituality today, *studies on Luke Acts.*

400 pages   paper $10.95
ISBN: 0-939680-03-3

TAPES BY MATTHEW FOX AND FRIENDS

One of the country's most popular retreat masters and spiritual guides has prepared an extraordinary cassette program.

+ MATTHEW FOX has prepared 15 complete tape programs rooted in a vision of a prayer life that has its flower in compassionate caring.

+ Jose Hobday, Msgr Robert Fox, Brian Swimme, MATT and other friends share their experience, strength and hope with you.

+ Spend a weekend with them . . . stretch them over days or weeks

+ Use them at home . . . lone, in a group . . . in a classroom, or in your car.

+ A fresh, imaginative, prayer resource you've been waiting for.

JUST RELEASED!

TAPE 15: Spirituality and Education

In this tape Matt Fox shares his insights into a Creation-Centered approach to education. He draws from his experiences as teacher/learner. He discounts the "Jacobs's ladder approach to education as doing something to another or superior interior relationships. He demonstrates concrete ways in which teachers and "students" can dance "Sarah's Circle" of compassion, caring, wisdom and inter-dependence. The discipline of reverencing life constitutes the heart of all human learning.

TAPE 14: Science, Spirituality and Education

Matt Fox dialogues with physicist/mathematician Dr. Brian Swimme in exploring the connection between the Mysteries of the Universe and Our Christian Spirituality. They describe their MANIFESTO (see this catalogue) for a global community. A renewed spirituality will allow a dialogue of science, education, and culture if religious faith will not seek its own perpetuation but will believe deeply enough that it can let go of its own privileged positions in order to be among the least and the poorest.

TAPE EIGHT: Holiness as Cosmic Hospitality

Pointing out that the meaning of holiness must be sought for our time. The theological explanation of hospitality, God as host, hostess, and the practical ramifications of hospitality to *self, others, nature* and *God.*

TAPE SEVEN: Images of Soul: psychology of spirituality

A terminal case of "left-brain-itis" haunts western civilization. Words have lost their moorings and meanings. Philosopher Charles Fair points out that when a civilization looses its meaning of "soul" that civilization dies. Today, in the west, we have lost the meaning of soul and we need to return to "right brain" insights for soul. These are expressed by images— out of new images of soul a new civilization can be born. Special attention is given to Meister Eckhart's images of soul.

TAPE SIX: Recovering Ritual in the West: liturgy & spirituality

A look at liturgy, music and ritual. An analysis of what's wrong in the west plus antidotes for healing. This analysis includes the absence of cosmos, body, social justice, and via negativa when westerners gather to worship. Antidotes for healing this malaise are noted with special attention paid to the prophetic role of music.

TAPE 13: Body as Metaphor

Jungian Analyst John Giannini and Matt Fox discuss the recovery of the holy trinity of Body, Soul, and Spirit. Eckhardt's wholistic, cosmic spirituality and Jung's principle of synchronicity heal the microcosm and macrocosm of western consciousness torn asunder by an ascetic dualism that pits spirit against matter.

TAPE 12: Creativity & Spirituality—a trialogue with Jose Hobday, Msgr. Robert Fox, and Matthew Fox. Street Priest, Msgr. Robert Fox of Harlem shares his experience of a creation-centered spirituality on the streets of New York. All three share that finding God in the midst of life is finding yourself, your neighbor, and all of creation and believing "it is good."

TAPE 11: An American Spirituality

Matt Fox believes that the phenomenon of prayer and interest in adult spirituality is clearly at the forefront of American culture today. In this tape he presents the forms this phenomenon takes and some of the reasons "why" we should not be surprised. Prayer as a cover up for injustice is dead. The quest of the American spirituality may be to end the CHAOS.

TAPE 10: A Native American Spirituality

Native American, Sister Jose Hobday dialogues with Matt Fox regarding the creation-centered tradition of the Native American Spirituality. Explored are images of soul, community, and person.

TAPE NINE: Social Justice, Art & Spirituality: a Holy Trinity and indivisible unity

Part and parcel of every unjust system is the separation of justice and art. Such separation renders art as mere entertainment or as investment for the powerful. Yet art remains the meaningful link between theory and social change; and between personal transformation & social transformation. This tape explores bringing the trinity of social justice, art and spirituality together again.

TAPE FIVE: Pleasure, Contemplation and Social Justice: antidote to the idolatry of consumerism

This meaning of contemplation as pleasure and savoring contemplation. This meaning of contemplation as pleasure and savoring contemplation . . . One reason why consumerism has taken such deep root in western culture is that western spiritualities have too often ignored a theology of pleasure. The Holy Spirit is discovered as the "Spirit of Transformation."

TAPE FOUR: Images of Compassion: East meets West

It seems that when you get to the roots of all major world spiritual traditions, they are all trying to teach people compassion. This tape examines four images found in all world religions to educate in compassion.

TAPE THREE: Psychology & Mysticism—Jung & Meister Eckhart

Jung admits his dependence on the great Dominican mystic Meister Eckhart when he writes that reading Meister Eckhart gave him "the key" to opening up the unconscious. This tape examines the insights into the human spirit uncovered by Meister Eckhart and Carl Gustave Jung: the importance of matter in our spiritual life.

TAPE TWO: Family Spirituality

The 1980's have been declared the decade of the family. This reflection considers three dimensions to family and spirituality: 1) The meaning of family with special attention to the cosmic family or "family of being" of which biblical tradition teaches; 2) Our family or local unit of intimacy as mystical energy source family as celebration; and 3) Our family or local unit of intimacy as a prophetic energy the family as a resistance unit.

TAPE ONE: From Climbing Jacob's Ladder to Dancing Sarah's Circle

A reflection on the change in mystical symbols from the overly competitive and self-centered "climbing Jacob's ladder" to the symbol of interdependence, creativity, humor and gentle Jung characterized by "Sarah's Circle."

WHEE! We, wee All the Way Home...

A GUIDE TO A SENSUAL PROPHETIC SPIRITUALITY.

Back in print with a completely new *Foreword to the 80s* by Matthew Fox.

"This book has excitement, color, swiftness and is service to the Church. WHEE! is a book for searchers into the meaning of life and revelation." *Review for Religious*

"WHEE! is provocative, exciting, and radical both in its scope and ideas. It is both socially relevant and psychologically sound."
Library Journal

"This is a pioneer book... a voyage replete with new ideas and seldom seen perspectives."
Thomasa F. O'Meara

"Constructive, humane, and joyful in its positive suggestions to improve life quality in a dangerously jaded world." Daniel Turner, National Association of Family Therapists and Counsellors.

264 pages   paper $8.95
ISBN: 0-938680-00-9

Qty	ORDER FORM	Each	Total
	Bear & Company "little magazine"	$15.00 yr	
	CANADIAN ORDERS: ADD $6.00 FOR PROCESSING		
	Western Spirituality	10.95	
	WHEE, We, wee	8.95	
	Psalms from the Hills of West Virginia	7.95	
	Meditations with Meister Eckhardt	6.95	
	Luke	10.95	
	Manifesto	3.50	
	Cash Total Books		
	TAPE ONE: Climbing/Dancing	7.95	
	TAPE TWO: Family Spirituality	7.95	
	TAPE THREE: Psychology & Mysticism	7.95	
	TAPE FOUR: Images of Compassion	7.95	
	TAPE FIVE: Pleasure, Contemplation, Justice	7.95	
	TAPE SIX: Recovering Ritual	7.95	
	TAPE SEVEN: Images of Soul	7.95	
	TAPE EIGHT: Holiness Cosmic Hospitality	7.95	
	TAPE NINE: Social Justice, ART, Spirituality	7.95	
	TAPE 10: A Native American Spirituality	7.95	
	TAPE 11: An American Spirituality	7.95	
	TAPE 12: A Spirituality for the Streets	7.95	
	TAPE 13: Body as Metaphor	7.95	
	TAPE 14: Science, Spirituality & Education	7.95	
	TAPE 15: Spirituality & Education	7.95	
	Cash Total Tapes		
	TOTAL TAPES & BOOKS		
	10% Handling & Shipping		
	TOTAL		

ALL MONIES MUST BE IN U.S. FUNDS ONLY
PAYABLE THROUGH A CONTINENTAL U.S. BANK

Check   Money Order   Visa   Mastercard

NAME _____

STREET _____

CITY _____ STATE _____ ZIP __

Card Number _____ Expires ___

Signature _____

MAIL YOUR ORDER TODAY TO: BEAR & COMPANY, INC.
6 Vista Grande Court   Santa Fe, NM 87501

PHONE TODAY: (505) 983-5968

Bear and Company, Inc.

publishes a complete line of creation centered spirituality materials by Matt Fox and associates.

+ Fine Books including: Whee! We, wee Western Spirituality
+ A "little magazine" : Bear & Company
+ Program materials including cassette tapes & spirit masters.

Order from your local bookstore. For the location of the store nearest you featuring Bear & Company or for a complete catalog please fill out this form or call (505) 983-5968.

To: Bear & Company, Inc.
6 Vista Grande Court
Santa Fe, NM 87501

Send to: _____
Street _____
City/State _____ Zip _____

☐ Please send me a catalog
☐ Put me on your mailing list
☐ Which store in my area carries Bear & Company materials
☐ I am interested in your "little Magazine"
☐ I am interested in program materials